THE

100 BEST STOCKS

TO

BUY IN AMERICA

2012

Martin F. Greene

ISBN 10: 1-4699-9585-9
ISBN 13: 978-1-4699-9585-4

This publication is designed to provide accurate and authoritative information with regard to the subject matter covered. It is sold with the understanding that the publisher is not engaged in rendering legal, accounting, or other professional advice. If legal advice or other expert assistance is required, the services of a competent professional person should be sought.

Dedication
To Marcus, Dianne, and Angel

TABLE OF CONTENTS

INTRODUCTION

Out of the thousands of stocks available for purchase only a small percentage have the right mix of stability, earning potential, and diversity to be worthy of investment. The way a company weathers the economics throughout its history speaks volumes as well as how its organization is structured to meet future demands. With detailed analysis a list of 100 stocks has been compiled to help an investor narrow their choice when the time comes to pick a stock for a portfolio. However, this book should only serve as a supplement when considering any stock for investment.

Factors such as risk and objectives also need to be addressed when considering an investment product. But with a little homework and careful evaluation of each stock considered, a structured portfolio of investments should take shape to help any investor accomplish their objectives.

Martin F. Greene
March 2012

THE

100 BEST STOCKS

TO

BUY IN AMERICA

The 100 STOCKS:

Company Name	Symbol	Sector
Abbott Laboratories	ABT	Health Care
Accenture PLC	ACN	Information Tech.
ACE Ltd.	ACE	Financials
AES Corp.	AES	Utilities
Aetna, Inc.	AET	Health Care
AFLAC, Inc.	AFL	Financials
Akamai Technologies, Inc.	AKAM	Information Tech.
Allegheny Tech., Inc.	ATI	Industrials
Altria Group, Inc.	MO	Consumer Goods
American Elec. Power Co.	AEP	Utilities
American Express, Co.	AXP	Financials
Amgen, Inc.	AMGN	Health Care
Applied Materials, Inc.	AMAT	Technology
Baxter International, Inc.	BAX	Health Care
Bed Bath & Beyond, Inc.	BBBY	Consumer Goods
BlackRock, Inc.	BLK	Financials
Boeing Co.	BA	Industrials
Brown-Forman Corp.	BF.B	Consumer Goods
Capital One Financial	COF	Financials
Cardinal Health, Inc.	CAH	Health Care
Chubb Corp.	CB	Financials
Cigna Corp.	CI	Health Care
Clorox Co.	CLX	Consumer Goods
Coca-Cola Co.	KO	Consumer Goods
Colgate-Palmolive Co.	CL	Consumer Goods
Corning, Inc.	GLW	Information Tech.
Covidien PLC	COV	Health Care
Cummins, Inc.	CMI	Industrials
CVS Caremark Corp.	CVS	Consumer Services
DaVita, Inc.	DVA	Health Care
Dell, Inc.	DELL	Information Tech.
Discover Financial Services	DFS	Financials
Dow Chemical Co.	DOW	Materials
Dr. Pepper Snapple Group	DPS	Consumer Goods
E. I. du Pont de Nemours	DD	Materials
Eastman Chemical Co.	EMN	Materials

Company Name	Symbol	Sector
EOG Resources, Inc.	EOG	Energy
Fastenal Co.	FAST	Industrials
FedEx Corp.	FDX	Industrials
Flowserve	FLS	Industrials
Ford Motor Co.	F	Consumer Goods
General Mills, Inc.	GIS	Consumer Goods
Goodyear Tire & Rubber	GT	Consumer Goods
W. W. Grainger, Inc.	GWW	Industrials
Halliburton Co.	HAL	Energy
Harris Corp.	HRS	Information Tech.
Inter. Business Machines	IBM	Information Tech.
Interpublic Group of Cos.	IPG	Consumer Services
Jacobs Engineering Group	JEC	Industrials
Joy Global, Inc.	JOY	Industrials
KLA-Tencor Corp.	KLAC	Information Tech.
Kohl's Corp.	KSS	Consumer Services
Lab. Corp. of America Hdgs.	LH	Health Care
Life Technologies Corp.	LIFE	Health Care
Lorillard, Inc.	LO	Consumer Goods
Masco Corp.	MAS	Industrials
McCormick & Co., Inc.	MKC	Consumer Goods
McDonald's Corp.	MCD	Consumer Services
McKesson Corp.	MCK	Health Care
Merck & Co., Inc.	MRK	Health Care
MetLife, Inc.	MET	Financials
Microsoft Corp.	MSFT	Information Tech.
Mosaic Co.	MOS	Materials
National Oilwell Varco, Inc.	NOV	Energy
Nordstrom, Inc.	JWN	Consumer Goods
Norfolk Southern Corp.	NSC	Industrials
Omnicom Group, Inc.	OMC	Consumer Services
ONEOK, Inc.	OKE	Utilities
Oracle Corp.	ORCL	Information Tech.
PACCAR, Inc.	PCAR	Industrials
Peabody Energy Corp.	BTU	Energy
PepsiCo, Inc.	PEP	Consumer Goods
Reynolds American, Inc.	RAI	Consumer Goods
Robert Half International	RHI	Industrials

Company Name	**Symbol**	**Sector**
Rockwell Automation, Inc.	ROK	Industrials
Sempra Energy	SRE	Utilities
Sigma-Aldrich Corp.	SIAL	Materials
Simon Property Group, Inc.	SPG	Financials
J. M. Smucker Co.	SJM	Consumer Goods
Southwest Airlines Co.	LUV	Industrials
Stanley Black & Decker	SWK	Industrials
Thermo Fisher Scientific	TMO	Health Care
Time Warner, Inc.	TWX	Consumer Services
Titanium Metals Corp.	TIE	Materials
United Parcel Service, Inc.	UPS	Industrials
U.S. Bancorp	USB	Financials
United Technologies Corp.	UTX	Industrials
Verizon Communications	VZ	Telecom. Services
V. F. Corp.	VFC	Consumer Goods
Walgreen Co.	WAG	Consumer Goods
Wal-Mart Stores, Inc.	WMT	Consumer Goods
Waste Management, Inc.	WM	Industrials
Waters Corp.	WAT	Health Care
Watson Pharmaceuticals	WPI	Health Care
Wells Fargo & Co.	WFC	Financials
Windstream Corp.	WIN	Telecom. Services
Wynn Resorts Ltd.	WYNN	Consumer Services
Xerox Corp.	XRX	Consumer Goods
Yahoo! Inc.	YHOO	Information Tech.
Zimmer Holdings, Inc.	ZMH	Health Care

ABBOTT LABORATORIES

Symbol: ABT (NYSE)
Price: $54.15 (as of 01/31/12)
Ratings:
   The Street: BUY
   Standard & Poor's: BUY ★ ★ ★ ★
   Ford Equity Research: BUY
Sector: Health Care
Industry: Pharmaceuticals
52-Week Range: $45.08 (02/01/11)-Low
                    $56.84 (01/04/12)-High
Shares Outstanding: 1.56B
Beta: .32
P/E (Trailing 12-Month): $17.99
EPS (Trailing 12-Month): $3.01
Annual Dividend per Share and Yield: $1.92/3.50%
Market Capitalization: $84.35B
Founded: 1888
Employees: 91,000
Website: http://www.abbott.com
Address:
Abbott Laboratories
100 Abbott Park Road
Abbott Park, IL 60064-6400
Phone: (847) 937-6100
Investor Relations:
Phone: (847) 937-8945

Company Summary: Abbott Laboratories is a diversified pharmaceuticals and health care products company which involves pharmaceuticals, medical devices and nutritional products. The company is divided into the following divisions: animal health; diabetes care; medical diagnostics; molecular analysis (DNA, RNA, etc.); nutrition (Similac, Isomil, Gain, Ensure, ZonePerfect and Glucerna); and vascular devices and technologies.

Revenue (Millions $)

Year	1st Q	2nd Q	3rd Q	4th Q	Year Total
2008:	6,766	7,314	7,498	7,950	29,528
2009:	6,718	7,495	7,761	8,790	30,765
2010:	7,698	8,826	8,675	9,968	35,167
2011:	9,041	9,616	9,817	10,377	38,851

Dividends (per share-last four)

$	Date Declared	Ex-Dividend Date	Date of Record	Payment Date
.48	02/18/11	04/13/11	04/15/11	05/16/11
.48	06/10/11	07/13/11	07/15/11	08/15/11
.48	09/15/11	10/12/11	10/14/11	11/15/11
.48	12/09/11	01/11/12	01/13/12	02/15/12

ACCENTURE PLC

Symbol: ACN (NYSE)
Price: $57.34 (as of 01/31/12)
Ratings:
    The Street: BUY
    Standard & Poor's: BUY ★ ★ ★ ★
    Ford Equity Research: HOLD
Sector: Information Technology
Industry: Information Technology and Consulting Services
52-Week Range: $47.40 (08/19/11)-Low
                    $63.66 (07/07/11)-High
Shares Outstanding: 647.21M
Beta: .82
P/E (Trailing 12-Month): $16.13
EPS (Trailing 12-Month): $3.55
Annual Dividend per Share and Yield: $1.35/2.40%
Market Capitalization: $37.11B
Founded: 1989 (as Andersen Consulting and Accenture in 2001)
Employees: 244,000
Website: http://www.accenture.com
Address: (Principal Executive Office)
Accenture PLC
1 Grand Canal Square
Grand Canal Harbour
Dublin, 2
Ireland - Map
Phone: +353 1 646 2000
Address: (U.S.)
Accenture PLC
1345 Avenue of the Americas
New York, NY 10105
Phone: (877) 889-9009
Investor Relations:
Phone: (877) 226-5659
E-mail: investor.relations@accenture.com

Company Summary: Accenture PLC is a management consulting, technology services and outsourcing company ranked as the largest consulting firm in the world.

Revenue (Millions $)

Year	1st Q	2nd Q	3rd Q	4th Q	Year Total
2008:	6,102	6,058	6,593	6,561	25,314
2009:	6,471	5,658	5,537	5,505	23,171
2010:	5,748	5,538	5,976	5,833	23,094
2011:	6,478	6,496	7,204	7,174	27,352

Dividends (per share-last four)

$	Date Declared	Ex-Dividend Date	Date of Record	Payment Date
.375	03/25/10	04/14/10	04/16/10	05/14/10
.45	09/29/10	10/13/10	10/15/10	11/15/10
.45	03/23/11	04/13/11	04/15/11	05/13/11
.675	09/26/11	10/12/11	10/14/11	11/15/11

ACE LTD.
Symbol: ACE (NYSE)
Price: $69.60 (as of 01/31/12)
Ratings:
>   **The Street:** BUY
>   **Standard & Poor's:** BUY ★ ★ ★ ★
>   **Ford Equity Research:** BUY

Sector: Financials
Industry: Property and Casualty Insurance
52-Week Range: $56.90 (10/04/11)-Low
> $73.76 (10/27/11)-High

Shares Outstanding: 336.82M
Beta: 1.05
P/E (Trailing 12-Month): $12.93
EPS (Trailing 12-Month): $5.38
Annual Dividend per Share and Yield: $1.88/2.70%
Market Capitalization: $23.44B
Founded: 1985
Employees: 16,000
Website: http://www.acelimited.com
Address: (Principal Executive Office)
Ace Ltd.
Barengasse 32
8001 Zurich
Switzerland
Phone: +41 0 43 456 7600
Address: (U.S.)
Ace Ltd.
1133 Avenue of the Americas
New York, NY 10036
Phone: (212) 827 4400
Investor Relations:
Phone: +1 441 299 9283 (Bermuda)
E-mail: investorrelations@acegroup.com
Company Summary: ACE Ltd. is a provider of insurance products covering property and casualty, accident and health, reinsurance, travel, creditor, and life insurance. The Company also offers services including process

management, unusual hazards identification and expected loss calculations, and engineering services.

Revenue (Millions $)

Year	1st Q	2nd Q	3rd Q	4th Q	Year Total
2008:	3,076	3,834	3,619	3,103	13,632
2009:	3,575	3,547	3,681	4,272	15,075
2010:	3,949	3,760	3,888	4,409	16,006
2011:	3,808	4,253	4,294	4,479	16,834

Dividends (per share-last four)

$	Date Declared	Ex-Dividend Date	Date of Record	Payment Date
.33	02/24/11	03/30/11	04/01/11	04/22/11
.35	05/18/11	06/28/11	06/30/11	07/21/11
.35	08/11/11	09/28/11	09/30/11	10/21/11
.47	11/17/11	01/10/12	01/10/12	01/31/12

AES CORP.

Symbol: AES (NYSE)
Price: $12.76 (as of 01/31/12)
Ratings:

The Street: HOLD
Standard & Poor's: BUY ★ ★ ★ ★
Ford Equity Research: HOLD

Sector: Utilities
Industry: Electric Utilities and Energy Traders
52-Week Range: $9.00 (10/04/11)-Low
$13.50 (04/08/11)-High
Shares Outstanding: 767.55M
Beta: 1.34
P/E (Trailing 12-Month): N/A
EPS (Trailing 12-Month): $-0.21
Annual Dividend per Share and Yield: N/A
Market Capitalization: $9.79B
Founded: 1981
Employees: 29,000
Website: http://www.aes.com
Address: (U.S.)
The AES Corp.
4300 Wilson Boulevard
11th Floor
Arlington, VA 22203
Phone: (703) 522-1315
Investor Relations:
Phone: (703) 682-6399
E-mail: invest@aes.com
Company Summary: The AES Corp. generates and distributes electrical power through the following subsidiaries: AES Eletropaulo, AES Gener, Premier Power, AES Energy Storage, AES Solar, AES Wind Generation, Indianapolis Power and Light Company and DPL, Inc.

Revenue (Millions $)

Year	1st Q	2nd Q	3rd Q	4th Q	Year Total
2008:	4,081	4,126	4,319	3,544	16,070
2009:	3,269	3,335	3,695	3,820	14,119
2010:	4,071	4,021	4,151	4,404	16,647
2011:	4,264	4,544	4,309	4,157	17,274

Dividends (per share-last)

$	Date Declared	Ex-Dividend Date	Date of Record	Payment Date
.8438	—	04/09/09	04/14/09	04/15/09

AETNA, INC.

Symbol: AET (NYSE)
Price: $43.70 (as of 01/31/12)
Ratings:
   The Street: BUY
   Standard & Poor's: BUY ★ ★ ★ ★
   Ford Equity Research: BUY
Sector: Health Care
Industry: Health Care Management
52-Week Range: $33.43 (10/04/11)-Low
                  $46.01 (05/19/11)-High
Shares Outstanding: 362.30M
Beta: .93
P/E (Trailing 12-Month): $9.30
EPS (Trailing 12-Month): $4.70
Annual Dividend per Share and Yield: $.70/1.60%
Market Capitalization: $15.83B
Founded: 1853
Employees: 34,000
Website: http://www.aetna.com
Address: (U.S.)
Aetna, Inc.
151 Farmington Avenue
Hartford, CT 06156
Phone: (860) 273-0123
Investor Relations:
Phone: (860)
E-mail: investorrelations@aetna.com
Company Summary: Aetna, Inc. provides traditional and consumer directed health care insurance products and related services, including medical, pharmaceutical, dental, behavioral health, group life, long-term care, disability plans, and medical management capabilities.

Revenue (Millions $)

Year	1st Q	2nd Q	3rd Q	4th Q	Year Total
2008:	7,739	7,828	7,625	7,759	30,951
2009:	8,615	8,671	8,722	8,756	34,764
2010:	8,622	8,546	8,539	8,540	34,246
2011:	8,388	8,344	8,475	8,544	33,751

Dividends (per share-last four)

$	Date Declared	Ex-Dividend Date	Date of Record	Payment Date
.15	02/03/11	04/12/11	04/14/11	04/29/11
.15	05/20/11	07/12/11	07/14/11	07/29/11
.15	09/23/11	10/11/11	10/13/11	10/28/11
.175	12/02/11	01/11/12	01/13/12	01/27/12

AFLAC, INC.

Symbol: AFL (NYSE)
Price: $48.23 (as of 01/31/12)
Ratings:
    The Street: BUY
    Standard & Poor's: BUY ★ ★ ★ ★
    Ford Equity Research: HOLD
Sector: Financial
Industry: Life and Health Insurance
52-Week Range: $31.25 (09/26/11)-Low
                     $59.54 (03/01/11)-High
Shares Outstanding: 466.31M
Beta: 2.53
P/E (Trailing 12-Month): $12.24
EPS (Trailing 12-Month): $3.94
Annual Dividend per Share and Yield: $1.32/2.70%
Market Capitalization: $22.51B
Founded: 1955
Employees: 7,900
Website: http://www.aflac.com
Address: (U.S.)
AFLAC, Inc.
1932 Wynnton Road
Columbus, GA 31999
Phone: (706) 323-3431
Investor Relations:
Phone: (800) 235 -2667
E-mail: ir@aflac.com
Company Summary: AFLAC, Inc. is the largest provider of supplemental health insurance in the United States and is the largest life insurer in Japan. The company is also a major player in payroll deduction insurance coverage, which pays cash benefits when a policyholder has a covered accident or illness.

Revenue (Millions $)

Year	1st Q	2nd Q	3rd Q	4th Q	Year Total
2008:	4,267	4,336	3,691	4,260	16,554
2009:	4,818	4,313	4,526	4,597	18,254
2010:	5,065	4,980	5,394	5,294	20,732
2011:	5,117	5,088	5,987	5,979	22,171

Dividends (per share-last four)

$	Date Declared	Ex-Dividend Date	Date of Record	Payment Date
.30	04/27/11	05/16/11	05/18/11	06/01/11
.30	07/27/11	08/15/11	08/17/11	09/01/11
.33	10/26/11	11/14/11	11/16/11	12/01/11
.33	01/31/12	02/13/12	02/15/12	03/01/12

AKAMAI TECHNOLOGIES, INC.

Symbol: AKAM (NASDAQ)
Price: $32.23 (as of 01/31/12)
Ratings:
    The Street: BUY
    Standard & Poor's: HOLD ★ ★ ★
    Ford Equity Research: HOLD
Sector: Information Technology
Industry: Internet Services
52-Week Range: $18.25 (10/04/11)-Low
                $43.58 (02/16/11)-High
Shares Outstanding: 179.43M
Beta: .30
P/E (Trailing 12-Month): $31.75
EPS (Trailing 12-Month): $1.01
Annual Dividend per Share and Yield: N/A
Market Capitalization: $5.78B
Founded: 1998
Employees: 2,200
Website: http://www.akamai.com
Address: (U.S.)
Akamai Technologies, Inc.
8 Cambridge Center
Cambridge, MA 02142
Phone: (617) 444-3000
Investor Relations:
Phone: (877) 565-7167
E-mail: Invrel@akamai.com
Company Summary: Akamai Technologies, Inc. is an Internet content delivery network which provides a service to companies that allows a more efficient delivery of information to users browsing the Web and downloading content.

Revenue (Millions $)

Year	1st Q	2nd Q	3rd Q	4th Q	Year Total
2008:	187.0	194.0	197.4	212.6	790.9
2009:	210.4	204.6	206.5	238.3	859.8
2010:	240.0	245.3	253.6	284.7	1,023.6
2011:	276.0	277.0	281.9	323.7	1,158.6

Dividends (none)

ALLEGHENY TECHNOLOGIES, INC.

Symbol: ATI (NYSE)
Price: $45.39 (as of 01/31/12)
Ratings:
   The Street: HOLD
   Standard & Poor's: HOLD ★ ★ ★
   Ford Equity Research: SELL
Sector: Industrials
Industry: Materials
52-Week Range: $30.79 (10/04/11)-Low
                $73.53 (04/27/11)-High
Shares Outstanding: 106.40M
Beta: 1.94
P/E (Trailing 12-Month): $23.06
EPS (Trailing 12-Month): $1.97
Annual Dividend per Share and Yield: $.72/1.50%
Market Capitalization: $4.83b
Founded: 1996 (by merger with Allegheny Ludlum Corp. and Teledyne, Inc.)
Employees: 11,400
Website: http://www.alleghenytechnologies.com
Address: (U.S.)
Allegheny Technologies, Inc.
1000 Six PPG Place
Pittsburgh, PA 15222-5479
Phone: (412) 394-2800
Investor Relations:
Phone: (412) 394-3004
E-mail: Dan.Greenfield@ATImetals.com
Company Summary: Allegheny Technologies, Inc. is a specialty metals company and is one of the largest and most diversified specialty metals producers in the world. The company's major markets are in aerospace, defense, oil and gas, the chemical process industry, electrical energy, and medical applications.

Revenue (Millions $)

Year	1st Q	2nd Q	3rd Q	4th Q	Year Total
2008:	1,343	1,461	1,392	1,113	5,310
2009:	832	710	698	816	3,055
2010:	899	1,052	1,059	1,038	4,048
2011:	1,227	1,352	1,353	1,251	5,183

Dividends (per share-last four)

$	Date Declared	Ex-Dividend Date	Date of Record	Payment Date
.18	02/25/11	03/09/11	03/11/11	03/29/11
.18	04/29/11	05/24/11	05/26/11	06/17/11
.18	09/09/11	09/16/11	09/20/11	09/28/11
.18	12/09/11	12/16/11	12/20/11	12/29/11

ALTRIA GROUP, INC.
Symbol: MO (NYSE)
Price: $28.40 (as of 01/31/12)
Ratings:
    The Street: BUY
    Standard & Poor's: BUY ★ ★ ★ ★
    Ford Equity Research: STRONG BUY
Sector: Consumer Goods
Industry: Tobacco
52-Week Range: $23.20 (08/09/11)-Low
                 $30.40 (12/21/11)-High
Shares Outstanding: 2.04B
Beta: .34
P/E (Trailing 12-Month): $17.32
EPS (Trailing 12-Month): $1.64
Annual Dividend per Share and Yield: $1.64/5.80%
Market Capitalization: $57.91B
Founded: 1985
Employees: 10,000
Website: http://www.altria.com
Address: (U.S.)
Altria Group, Inc.
6601 West Broad Street
Richmond, VA 23230
Phone: (804) 274-2200
Investor Relations:
Phone: (804) 484-8222
Company Summary: Altria Group, Inc. (previously named Philip Morris Companies, Inc.) specializes in a variety of tobacco products.

Revenue (Millions $)

Year	1ˢᵗ Q	2ⁿᵈ Q	3ʳᵈ Q	4ᵗʰ Q	Year Total
2008:	4,410	5,054	5,238	4,654	19,357
2009:	4,523	6,719	6,300	6,014	23,556
2010:	5,760	6,274	6,402	5,927	24,363
2011:	5,643	5,920	6,108	6,129	23,800

Dividends (per share-last four)

$	Date Declared	Ex-Dividend Date	Date of Record	Payment Date
.38	02/24/11	03/11/11	03/15/11	04/11/11
.38	05/19/11	06/13/11	06/15/11	07/11/11
.41	08/26/11	09/13/11	09/15/11	10/11/11
.41	12/14/11	12/22/11	12/27/11	01/10/12

AMERICAN ELECTRIC POWER CO., INC.

Symbol: AEP (NYSE)
Price: $39.56 (as of 01/31/12)
Ratings:
 The Street: BUY
 Standard & Poor's: HOLD ★ ★ ★
 Ford Equity Research: HOLD
Sector: Utilities
Industry: Electric Utilities
52-Week Range: $33.09 (08/09/11)-Low
        $41.98 (01/03/12)-High
Shares Outstanding: 303.12M
Beta: .40
P/E (Trailing 12-Month): $10.52
EPS (Trailing 12-Month): $3.76
Annual Dividend per Share and Yield: $1.88/4.70%
Market Capitalization: $19.10B
Founded: 1906
Employees: 18,712
Website: http://www.aep.com
Address: (U.S.)
American Electric Power Co., Inc.
1 Riverside Plaza
Columbus, OH 43215-2372
Phone: (614) 716-1000
Investor Relations:
Phone: (614) 716-2819
Company Summary: American Electric Power Co., Inc. is an electric utility that ranks among the nation's largest generators of electricity. The company also owns the nation's largest electricity transmission system, which consist of a 39,000-mile network.

Revenue (Millions $)

Year	1st Q	2nd Q	3rd Q	4th Q	Year Total
2008:	3,467	3,546	4,191	3,236	14,440
2009:	3,458	3,202	3,547	3,282	13,489
2010:	3,569	3,360	4,064	3,434	14,427
2011:	3,730	3,609	4,333	3,444	15,116

Dividends (per share-last four)

$	Date Declared	Ex-Dividend Date	Date of Record	Payment Date
.46	04/26/11	05/06/11	05/10/11	06/10/11
.46	07/27/11	08/08/11	08/10/11	09/09/11
.47	10/25/11	11/08/11	11/10/11	12/09/11
.47	01/25/12	02/08/12	02/10/12	03/09/12

AMERICAN EXPRESS CO.

Symbol: AXP (NYSE)
Price: $50.14 (as of 01/31/12)
Ratings:
    The Street: BUY
    Standard & Poor's: STRONG BUY ★ ★ ★ ★ ★
    Ford Equity Research: STRONG BUY
Sector: Financials
Industry: Credit Finance
52-Week Range: $41.30 (10/04/11)-Low
                    $53.80 (07/07/11)-High
Shares Outstanding: 1.16B
Beta: 2.0
P/E (Trailing 12-Month): $12.17
EPS (Trailing 12-Month): $4.12
Annual Dividend per Share and Yield: $.72/1.40%
Market Capitalization: $58.36B
Founded: 1850
Employees: 62,500
Website: http://www.americanexpress.com
Address: (U.S.)
American Express Co.
World Financial Center
200 Vesey Street
New York, NY 10285-3106
Phone: (212) 640-2000
Investor Relations:
Phone: (212) 640-2000
E-mail: IR@aexp.com
Company Summary: American Express Co. is a financial services company which is a major player in credit card, charge card, and traveler's cheque businesses.

Revenue (Millions $)

Year	1st Q	2nd Q	3rd Q	4th Q	Year Total
2008:	8,105	8,340	8,007	7,468	31,920
2009:	6,481	6,639	6,559	7,051	26,730
2010:	7,204	7,468	7,033	7,322	29,027
2011:	7,031	7,618	8,146	8,317	31,112

Dividends (per share-last four)

$	Date Declared	Ex-Dividend Date	Date of Record	Payment Date
.18	03/28/11	04/06/11	04/08/11	05/10/11
.18	05/23/11	06/29/11	07/01/11	08/10/11
.18	09/21/11	10/05/11	10/07/11	11/10/11
.18	11/22/11	01/04/12	01/06/12	02/10/12

AMGEN, INC.

Symbol: AMGN (NASDAQ)
Price: $67.93 (as of 01/31/12)
Ratings:
    The Street: BUY
    Standard & Poor's: BUY ★ ★ ★ ★
    Ford Equity Research: STRONG BUY
Sector: Health Care
Industry: Biotechnology
52-Week Range: $47.66 (08/11/11)-Low
                     $69.63 (01/20/12)-High
Shares Outstanding: 796.00M
Beta: .60
P/E (Trailing 12-Month): $16.81
EPS (Trailing 12-Month): $4.04
Annual Dividend per Share and Yield: $1.44/2.10%
Market Capitalization: $54.07B
Founded: 1980
Employees: 17,000
Website: http://www.amgen.com
Address: (U.S.)
Amgen, Inc.
One Amgen Center Drive
Thousand Oaks, CA 91320-1799
Phone: (805) 447-1000
Investor Relations:
Phone: (805) 447-1060
E-mail: investor.relations@amgen.com
Company Summary: Amgen, Inc. is a biotechnology company and ranks as the world's largest independent biotech firm. The company's major products are Epogen, Aranesp, Enbrel, Kineret, Neulasta, Neupogen, Sensipar/Mimpara, Nplate, Vectibix, Prolia and XGEVA.

Revenue (Millions $)

Year	1st Q	2nd Q	3rd Q	4th Q	Year Total
2008:	3,613	3,764	3,875	3,751	15,003
2009:	3,308	3,713	3,812	3,809	14,642
2010:	3,592	3,804	3,816	3,841	15,053
2011:	3,706	3,959	3,944	3,973	15,582

Dividends (per share-last three)

$	Date Declared	Ex-Dividend Date	Date of Record	Payment Date
.28	07/28/11	08/16/11	08/18/11	09/08/11
.28	10/13/11	11/15/11	11/17/11	12/08/11
.36	12/15/11	02/13/12	02/15/12	03/07/12

APPLIED MATERIALS, INC.

Symbol: AMAT (NASDAQ)
Price: $12.27 (as of 01/31/12)
Ratings:
    The Street: BUY
    Standard & Poor's: STRONG BUY ★ ★ ★ ★ ★
    Ford Equity Research: HOLD
Sector: Technology
Industry: Semiconductor Equipment
52-Week Range: $9.70 (10/04/11)-Low
                 $16.93 (03/03/11)-High
Shares Outstanding: 1.31B
Beta: 1.3
P/E (Trailing 12-Month): $8.47
EPS (Trailing 12-Month): $1.45
Annual Dividend per Share and Yield: $.32/2.60%
Market Capitalization: $16.03B
Founded: 1967
Employees: 12,900
Website: http://www.appliedmaterials.com
Address: (U.S.)
Applied Materials, Inc.
3050 Bowers Avenue
Santa Clara, CA 95052-8039
Phone: (408) 727-5555
Investor Relations:
Phone: (408) 748-5227
E-mail: Investor_Relations@amat.com
Company Summary: Applied Materials, Inc. is an equipment producer serving the semiconductor, TFT LCD display, Glass, WEB and solar (crystalline and thin film) manufacturing industries. The company also creates and commercializes nanomanufacturing technology.

Revenue (Millions $)

Year	1st Q	2nd Q	3rd Q	4th Q	Year Total
2008:	2,087	2,150	1,848	2,044	8,129
2009:	1,333	1,020	1,134	1,526	5,014
2010:	1,849	2,296	2,518	2,886	9,549
2011:	2,686	2,862	2,787	2,182	10,517

Dividends (per share-last four)

$	Date Declared	Ex-Dividend Date	Date of Record	Payment Date
.08	03/08/11	05/27/11	06/01/11	06/22/11
.08	06/06/11	08/29/11	08/31/11	09/21/11
.08	09/13/11	11/21/11	11/23/11	12/14/11
.08	12/06/11	02/21/12	02/23/12	03/15/12

BAXTER INTERNATIONAL, INC.

Symbol: BAX (NYSE)
Price: $55.48 (as of 01/31/12)
Ratings:

  The Street: BUY
  Standard & Poor's: BUY ★ ★ ★ ★
  Ford Equity Research: HOLD
Sector: Health Care
Industry: Medical Supplies
52-Week Range: $47.55 (12/19/11)-Low
                $62.50 (07/21/11)-High
Shares Outstanding: 563.87M
Beta: .46
P/E (Trailing 12-Month): $14.30
EPS (Trailing 12-Month): $3.88
Annual Dividend per Share and Yield: $1.34/2.40%
Market Capitalization: $31.28B
Founded: 1931
Employees: 48,000
Website: http://www.baxter.com
Address: (U.S.)
Baxter International, Inc.
One Baxter Parkway
Deerfield, IL 60015-4633
Phone: (847) 948-2000
Investor Relations:
Phone: (847) 948-3371
Company Summary: Baxter International, Inc. is a health care company that offers products to treat hemophilia, kidney disease, immune disorders and other chronic and acute medical conditions. The company has three manufacturing divisions: Bioscience (producing recombinant and blood plasma proteins to treat hemophilia and other bleeding disorders; Medication Delivery (producing intravenous solutions and other products used in the delivery of fluids and drugs to patients); and Renal (providing products to treat end-stage renal disease).

Revenue (Millions $)

Year	1st Q	2nd Q	3rd Q	4th Q	Year Total
2008:	2,877	3,189	3,151	3,131	12,348
2009:	2,824	3,123	3,145	3,470	12,562
2010:	2,927	3,194	3,224	3,498	12,843
2011:	3,284	3,536	3,479	3,594	13,893

Dividends (per share-last four)

$	Date Declared	Ex-Dividend Date	Date of Record	Payment Date
.31	02/15/11	03/08/11	03/10/11	04/01/11
.31	05/02/11	06/08/11	06/10/11	07/01/11
.31	07/26/11	09/07/11	09/09/11	10/03/11
.335	11/15/11	12/07/11	12/09/11	01/04/12

BED BATH & BEYOND, INC.

Symbol: BBBY (NASDAQ)
Price: $60.70 (as of 01/31/12)
Ratings:
    The Street: BUY
    Standard & Poor's: BUY ★ ★ ★ ★
    Ford Equity Research: STRONG BUY
Sector: Consumer Goods
Industry: Home Furnishings
52-Week Range: $44.79 (03/16/11)-Low
                  $63.83 (11/08/11)-High
Shares Outstanding: 236.75M
Beta: 1.1
P/E (Trailing 12-Month): $16.25
EPS (Trailing 12-Month): $3.74
Annual Dividend per Share and Yield: N/A
Market Capitalization: $14.37B
Founded: 1971
Employees: 45,000
Website: http://www.bedbathandbeyond.com
Address: (U.S.)
Bed Bath & Beyond, Inc.
650 Liberty Avenue
Union, NJ 07083
Phone: (908) 688-0888
Investor Relations:
Phone: (908) 855-4554
Company Summary: Bed Bath & Beyond, Inc. operates a chain of retail stores in the United States, Puerto Rico and Canada. The company primarily sells merchandise tailored for the bedroom, bathroom, kitchen and dining room.

Revenue (Millions $)

Year	1st Q	2nd Q	3rd Q	4th Q	Year Total
2008:	1,553	1,768	1,795	1,933	7,049
2009:	1,648	1,854	1,783	1,923	7,208
2010:	1,694	1,915	1,975	2,244	7,829
2011:	1,923	2,137	2,194	2,505	8,759
2012:	2,110	2,314	2,344	—	—

Dividends (none)

BLACKROCK, INC.

Symbol: BLK (NYSE)
Price: $182.00 (as of 01/31/12)
Ratings:
  The Street: BUY
  Standard & Poor's: HOLD ★ ★ ★
  Ford Equity Research: HOLD
Sector: Financials
Industry: Asset Management
52-Week Range: $137.00 (10/04/11)-Low
         $209.77 (03/01/11)-High
Shares Outstanding: 178.31M
Beta: 1.53
P/E (Trailing 12-Month): $14.71
EPS (Trailing 12-Month): $12.37
Annual Dividend per Share and Yield: $5.50/2.90%
Market Capitalization: $32.45B
Founded: 1998
Employees: 10,100
Website: http://www.blackrock.com
Address: (U.S.)
BlackRock, Inc.
Park Avenue Plaza
55 East 52nd Street
New York, NY 10055
Phone: (212) 810-5300
Investor Relations:
E-mail: invrel@blackrock.com
Company Summary: BlackRock, Inc. is an investment management corporation and ranks as the world's largest asset manager. The company provides investment, advisory, and risk management solutions.

Revenue (Millions $)

Year	1st Q	2nd Q	3rd Q	4th Q	Year Total
2008:	1,300	1,387	1,313	1,064	5,064
2009:	987	1,029	1,140	1,544	4,700
2010:	1,995	2,032	2,092	2,493	8,612
2011:	2,282	2,347	2,225	2,227	9,081

Dividends (per share-last four)

$	Date Declared	Ex-Dividend Date	Date of Record	Payment Date
1.375	02/24/11	03/03/11	03/07/11	03/23/11
1.375	05/25/11	06/03/11	06/07/11	06/23/11
1.375	06/22/11	08/31/11	09/02/11	09/22/11
1.375	09/27/11	12/01/11	12/05/11	12/23/11

BOEING CO.

Symbol: BA (NYSE)
Price: $74.18 (as of 01/31/12)
Ratings:
> **The Street:** BUY
> **Standard & Poor's:** BUY ★ ★ ★ ★
> **Ford Equity Research:** HOLD

Sector: Industrials
Industry: Aerospace and Defense Services
52-Week Range: $56.01 (08/11/11)-Low
$80.65 (05/02/11)-High
Shares Outstanding: 745.72M
Beta: 1.27
P/E (Trailing 12-Month): $13.89
EPS (Trailing 12-Month): $5.34
Annual Dividend per Share and Yield: $1.76/2.40%
Market Capitalization: $55.24B
Founded: 1916
Employees: 171,700
Website: http://www.boeing.com
Address: (U.S.)
The Boeing Co.
100 North Riverside Plaza
Chicago, IL 60606-1596
Phone: (312) 544-2000
Investor Relations:
Phone: (312) 544-2000
Company Summary: The Boeing Co. is an aerospace and defense corporation that merged with McDonnell Douglas in 1997. The company has the following divisions: Boeing Commercial Airplanes; Boeing Defense, Space and Security; Engineering, Operations and Technology; Boeing Capital; and Boeing Shared Services Group.

Revenue (Millions $)

Year	1st Q	2nd Q	3rd Q	4th Q	Year Total
2008:	15,990	16,962	15,293	12,664	60,909
2009:	16,502	14,296	16,688	17,937	65,423
2010:	15,216	15,573	16,967	16,550	64,306
2011:	14,910	16,543	17,727	19,555	68,735

Dividends (per share-last four)

$	Date Declared	Ex-Dividend Date	Date of Record	Payment Date
.42	05/02/11	05/11/11	05/13/11	06/03/11
.42	06/27/11	08/10/11	08/12/11	09/02/11
.42	10/31/11	11/08/11	11/11/11	12/02/11
.44	12/12/11	02/08/12	02/10/12	03/02/12

BROWN-FORMAN CORP.

Symbol: BF.B (Class B shares-NYSE)
Price: $81.21 (as of 01/31/12)
Ratings:
  The Street: N/A
  Standard & Poor's: BUY ★ ★ ★ ★
  Ford Equity Research: HOLD
Sector: Consumer Goods
Industry: Wineries and Distillers
52-Week Range: $62.14 (08/10/11)-Low
            $83.53 (01/26/12)-High
Shares Outstanding: 141.91M
Beta: .59
P/E (Trailing 12-Month): $20.29
EPS (Trailing 12-Month): $4.00
Annual Dividend per Share and Yield: $1.40/1.70%
Market Capitalization: $11.52B
Founded: 1870
Employees: 4,120
Website: http://www.brown-forman.com
Address: (U.S.)
Brown-Forman Corp.
850 Dixie Highway
Louisville, KY 40210
Phone: (502) 585-1100
Investor Relations:
Phone: (502) 774-7325
E-mail: Investor_Relations@b-f.com
Company Summary: The Brown-Forman Corp. is a distiller and vintner. The company's brands include Jack Daniel's, Southern Comfort, Finlandia Vodka, Woodford Reserve Bourbon, Canadian Mist, Early Times, Old Forester, and Korbel champagne.

Revenue (Millions $)

Year	1st Q	2nd Q	3rd Q	4th Q	Year Total
2008:	739	893	877	772	3,281
2009:	790	935	784	683	3,192
2010:	738	893	862	733	3,226
2011:	745	906	962	791	3,404
2012:	840	1,014	959	—	—

Dividends (per share-last four)

$	Date Declared	Ex-Dividend Date	Date of Record	Payment Date
.32	05/26/11	06/06/11	06/08/11	07/01/11
.32	07/28/11	09/01/11	09/06/11	10/03/11
.35	11/17/11	12/02/11	12/06/11	12/27/11
.35	01/24/12	03/01/11	03/05/12	04/02/12

CAPITAL ONE FINANCIAL CORP.

Symbol: COF (NYSE)
Price: $45.75 (as of 01/31/12)
Ratings:
   The Street: BUY
   Standard & Poor's: BUY ★ ★ ★ ★
   Ford Equity Research: HOLD
Sector: Financials
Industry: Banking and Credit Services
52-Week Range: $35.94 (08/08/11)-Low
                   $56.26 (05/19/11)-High
Shares Outstanding: 456.40M
Beta: 2.17
P/E (Trailing 12-Month): $6.73
EPS (Trailing 12-Month): $6.80
Annual Dividend per Share and Yield: $.20/.40%
Market Capitalization: $20.88B
Founded: 1988
Employees: 30,500
Website: http://www.capitalone.com
Address: (U.S.)
Capital One Financial Corp.
1680 Capital One Drive
McLean, VA 22102
Phone: (703) 720-1000
Investor Relations:
E-mail: investor.relations@capitalone.com
Company Summary: Capital One Financial Corp. is a bank holding company specializing in credit cards, home loans, auto loans, banking and savings products.

Revenue (Millions $)

Year	1st Q	2nd Q	3rd Q	4th Q	Year Total
2008:	4,936	4,269	4,469	4,137	17,811
2009:	3,740	3,949	4,255	4,007	15,951
2010:	5,091	4,642	4,722	4,613	19,067
2011:	4,694	4,556	4,706	4,569	18,525

Dividends (per share-last four)

$	Date Declared	Ex-Dividend Date	Date of Record	Payment Date
.05	05/11/11	05/19/11	05/23/11	06/03/11
.05	07/28/11	08/10/11	08/12/11	08/22/11
.05	11/11/11	11/17/11	11/21/11	12/02/11
.05	01/31/12	02/08/12	02/10/12	02/21/12

CARDINAL HEALTH, INC.

Symbol: CAH (NYSE)
Price: $43.03 (as of 01/31/12)
Ratings:
    The Street: BUY
    Standard & Poor's: BUY ★ ★ ★ ★
    Ford Equity Research: STRONG BUY
Sector: Health Care
Industry: Wholesale Distributors
52-Week Range: $37.53 (08/09/11)-Low
                  $47.06 (07/07/11)-High
Shares Outstanding: 345.68M
Beta: .57
P/E (Trailing 12-Month): $16.82
EPS (Trailing 12-Month): $2.56
Annual Dividend per Share and Yield: $.86/2.00%
Market Capitalization: $14.87B
Founded: 1971 (as Cardinal Foods)
Employees: 31,900
Website: http://www.cardinalhealth.com
Address: (U.S.)
Cardinal Health, Inc.
7000 Cardinal Place
Dublin, OH 43017
Phone: (614) 757-5000
Investor Relations:
Phone: (614) 757-5000
Company Summary: Cardinal Health, Inc. is a health care services company that specializes in the distribution of pharmaceuticals and medical products. The company also manufactures medical, surgical and fluid management products.

Revenue (Millions $)

Year	1st Q	2nd Q	3rd Q	4th Q	Year Total
2008:	21,973	23,283	22,910	22,926	91,091
2009:	24,321	25,075	24,918	25,199	99,512
2010:	24,781	24,920	24,343	24,460	98,503
2011:	24,438	25,372	26,071	26,764	102,644
2012:	26,972	27,078	—	—	—

Dividends (per share-last four)

$	Date Declared	Ex-Dividend Date	Date of Record	Payment Date
.215	05/04/11	06/29/11	07/01/11	07/15/11
.215	08/03/11	09/28/11	10/01/11	10/15/11
.215	11/02/11	12/28/11	01/01/12	01/15/11
.215	02/07/12	03/28/11	04/01/12	04/15/12

CHUBB CORP.

Symbol: CB (NYSE)
Price: $67.41 (as of 01/31/12)
Ratings:
  The Street: BUY
  Standard & Poor's: HOLD ★ ★ ★ ☆ ☆
  Ford Equity Research: HOLD
Sector: Financials
Industry: Property and Casualty Insurance
52-Week Range: $55.39 (08/08/11)-Low
               $71.76 (01/23/12)-High
Shares Outstanding: 272.50M
Beta: .67
P/E (Trailing 12-Month): $11.70
EPS (Trailing 12-Month): $5.76
Annual Dividend per Share and Yield: $1.56/2.30%
Market Capitalization: $18.37B
Founded: 1882 (as Chubb & Son, 1967 as the Chubb Corp.)
Employees: 10,100
Website: http://www.chubb.com
Address: (U.S.)
The Chubb Corp.
15 Mountain View Road
Warren, NJ 07059
Phone: (908) 903-2000
Investor Relations:
Phone: (908) 903-2365
Company Summary: The Chubb Corp. engages in commercial, specialty, surety, and personal insurance services. The company ranks as the 11th largest property and casualty insurer in the United States.

Revenue (Millions $)

Year	1st Q	2nd Q	3rd Q	4th Q	Year Total
2008:	3,489	3,354	3,303	3,075	13,221
2009:	2,965	3,266	3,320	3,465	13,016
2010:	3,323	3,318	3,267	3,411	13,319
2011:	3,420	3,400	3,420	3,345	13,585

Dividends (per share-last four)

$	Date Declared	Ex-Dividend Date	Date of Record	Payment Date
.39	06/09/11	06/22/11	06/24/11	07/12/11
.39	09/08/11	09/21/11	09/23/11	10/11/11
.39	12/08/11	12/21/11	12/23/11	01/10/11
.41	02/23/12	03/14/12	03/16/12	04/03/12

CIGNA CORP.
Symbol: CI (NYSE)
Price: $44.83 (as of 01/31/12)
Ratings:
>   **The Street:** BUY
>   **Standard & Poor's:** BUY ★ ★ ★ ★
>   **Ford Equity Research:** HOLD

Sector: Health Care
Industry: Managed Health Care Plans
52-Week Range: $38.79 (10/04/11)-Low
$52.95 (07/21/11)-High
Shares Outstanding: 270.22M
Beta: .75
P/E (Trailing 12-Month): $8.16
EPS (Trailing 12-Month): $5.50
Annual Dividend per Share and Yield: $.04/.10%
Market Capitalization: $12.11B
Founded: 1792 (as the Insurance Company of North America and in 1982 by merger of the Cigna Corp. and Connecticut General Life Insurance Company)
Employees: 30,000
Website: http://www.cigna.com
Address: (U.S.)
Cigna Corp.
900 Cottage Grove Road
Bloomfield, CT 06002
Phone: (860) 226-6000
Investor Relations:
Phone: (215) 761-1414
E-mail: edwin.detrick@cigna.com
Company Summary: The Cigna Corp. is a health services company and provides administrative services only, not insurance, to approximately 80 percent of its clients.

Revenue (Millions $)

Year	1st Q	2nd Q	3rd Q	4th Q	Year Total
2008:	4,569	4,863	4,852	4,817	19,101
2009:	4,773	4,488	4,517	4,636	18,414
2010:	5,205	5,353	5,266	5,429	21,253
2011:	5,413	5,509	5,613	5,463	21,998

Dividends (per share-last four)

$	Date Declared	Ex-Dividend Date	Date of Record	Payment Date
.04	02/25/09	03/09/09	03/11/09	04/10/09
.04	02/24/10	03/09/10	03/11/10	04/12/10
.04	02/23/11	03/09/11	03/11/11	04/11/11
.04	02/22/12	03/08/12	03/12/12	04/10/12

CLOROX CO.

Symbol: CLX (NYSE)
Price: $68.66 (as of 01/31/12)
Ratings:
> **The Street:** HOLD
> **Standard & Poor's:** HOLD ★ ★ ★
> **Ford Equity Research:** HOLD

Sector: Consumer Goods
Industry: Household Products
52-Week Range: $63.06 (11/23/11)-Low
$75.44 (07/20/11)-High
Shares Outstanding: 129.80M
Beta: .47
P/E (Trailing 12-Month): $19.79
EPS (Trailing 12-Month): $3.47
Annual Dividend per Share and Yield: $2.40/3.50%
Market Capitalization: $9.06B
Founded: 1913 (as the Electro-Alkaline Company)
Employees: 8,100
Website: http://www.thecloroxcompany.com
Address: (U.S.)
The Clorox Co.
1221 Broadway
Oakland, CA 94612-1888
Phone: (510) 271-7000
Investor Relations:
Phone: (888) 259-6973
E-mail: clorox.investor.relations@clorox.com
Company Summary: The Clorox Co. manufactures various food and chemical products and is best known for its bleach products carrying the Clorox name.

Revenue (Millions $)

Year	1st Q	2nd Q	3rd Q	4th Q	Year Total
2008:	1,239	1,186	1,353	1,495	5,273
2009:	1,384	1,216	1,350	1,500	5,450
2010:	1,372	1,279	1,366	1,517	5,534
2011:	1,266	1,179	1,304	1,482	5,231
2012:	1,305	1,221	—	—	—

Dividends (per share-last four)

$	Date Declared	Ex-Dividend Date	Date of Record	Payment Date
.60	05/18/11	07/25/11	07/27/11	08/12/11
.60	09/13/11	10/24/11	10/26/11	11/14/11
.60	11/15/11	01/24/12	01/26/12	02/13/12
.60	02/14/12	04/23/12	04/25/12	05/11/12

COCA-COLA CO.

Symbol: KO (NYSE)
Price: $67.53 (as of 01/31/12)
Ratings:
   The Street: BUY
   Standard & Poor's: STRONG BUY ★ ★ ★ ★ ★
   Ford Equity Research: HOLD
Sector: Consumer Goods
Industry: Soft Drinks
52-Week Range: $61.29 (03/16/11)-Low
                  $71.77 (09/08/11)-High
Shares Outstanding: 2.26B
Beta: .49
P/E (Trailing 12-Month): $12.42
EPS (Trailing 12-Month): $5.44
Annual Dividend per Share and Yield: $1.88/2.80%
Market Capitalization: $153.38B
Founded: 1892
Employees: 139,600
Website: http://www.cocacola.com
Address: (U.S.)
The Coca-Cola Co.
One Coca-Cola Plaza
Atlanta, GA 30313
Phone: (404) 676-2121
Investor Relations:
Phone: (800) 468-7856
Company Summary: The Coca-Cola Co. is a beverage manufacturer, retailer and marketer of non-alcoholic beverage concentrates and syrups. The company is best known for its flagship beverage, Coca-Cola, invented in 1886.

Revenue (Millions $)

Year	1st Q	2nd Q	3rd Q	4th Q	Year Total
2008:	7,379	9,046	8,393	7,126	31,944
2009:	7,169	8,267	8,044	7,510	30,990
2010:	7,525	8,674	8,426	10,494	35,119
2011:	10,517	12,737	12,248	11,040	46,542

Dividends (per share-last four)

$	Date Declared	Ex-Dividend Date	Date of Record	Payment Date
.47	04/28/11	06/13/11	06/15/11	07/01/11
.47	07/21/11	09/13/11	09/15/11	10/01/11
.47	10/20/11	11/29/11	12/01/11	12/15/11
.51	02/16/12	03/13/12	03/15/12	04/01/12

COLGATE-PALMOLIVE CO.

Symbol: CL (NYSE)
Price: $90.72 (as of 01/31/12)
Ratings:
    The Street: BUY
    Standard & Poor's: HOLD ★ ★ ★ ☆ ☆
    Ford Equity Research: HOLD
Sector: Consumer Goods
Industry: Household Products
52-Week Range: $76.39 (03/18/11)-Low
                $94.89 (09/20/11)-High
Shares Outstanding: 479.58M
Beta: .38
P/E (Trailing 12-Month): $18.36
EPS (Trailing 12-Month): $4.94
Annual Dividend per Share and Yield: $2.32/2.60%
Market Capitalization: $43.86B
Founded: 1806
Employees: 39,200
Website: http://www.colgate.com
Address: (U.S.)
Colgate-Palmolive Co.
300 Park Avenue
New York City, NY 10022
Phone: (212) 310-2000
Investor Relations:
Phone: (212) 310-2575
E-mail: Investor_Relations@colpal.com
Company Summary: The Colgate-Palmolive Co. is a consumer products company focused on the production, distribution and provision of household, health care and personal products, such as soaps, detergents, and oral hygiene products. The company, under its Hill's brand, also manufactures veterinary products.

Revenue (Millions $)

Year	1st Q	2nd Q	3rd Q	4th Q	Year Total
2008:	3,713	3,965	3,988	3,664	15,330
2009:	3,503	3,745	3,998	4,081	15,327
2010:	3,829	3,814	3,943	3,978	15,564
2011:	3,994	4,185	4,383	4,172	16,734

Dividends (per share-last four)

$	Date Declared	Ex-Dividend Date	Date of Record	Payment Date
.58	02/24/11	04/22/11	04/26/11	05/16/11
.58	07/14/11	07/22/11	07/26/11	08/15/11
.58	10/13/11	10/21/11	10/25/11	11/15/11
.58	01/12/12	01/20/12	01/24/12	02/15/12

CORNING, INC.

Symbol: GLW (NYSE)
Price: $12.87 (as of 01/31/12)
Ratings:
    The Street: HOLD
    Standard & Poor's: HOLD ★ ★ ★ ☆ ☆
    Ford Equity Research: HOLD
Sector: Information Technology
Industry: Electronics
52-Week Range: $11.51 (10/04/11)-Low
                $23.12 (03/07/11)-High
Shares Outstanding: 1.52B
Beta: 1.23
P/E (Trailing 12-Month): $7.27
EPS (Trailing 12-Month): $1.77
Annual Dividend per Share and Yield: $.30/2.40%
Market Capitalization: $19.50B
Founded: 1851
Employees: 26,200
Website: http://www.corning.com
Address: (U.S.)
Corning, Inc.
One Riverfront Plaza
Corning, NY 14831
Phone: (607) 974-9000
Investor Relations:
Phone: (888) 267-6464
Email: irinfo@corning.com
Company Summary: Corning, Inc. is a manufacturer of glass, ceramics and related materials, primarily for industrial and electronic applications.

Revenue (Millions $)

Year	1st Q	2nd Q	3rd Q	4th Q	Year Total
2008:	1,617	1,692	1,555	1,084	5,948
2009:	989	1,395	1,479	1,532	5,395
2010:	1,553	1,712	1,602	1,765	6,632
2011:	1,923	2,005	2,075	1,887	7,890

Dividends (per share-last four)

$	Date Declared	Ex-Dividend Date	Date of Record	Payment Date
.05	04/27/11	05/26/11	05/31/11	06/30/11
.05	07/20/11	08/29/11	08/31/11	09/30/11
.075	10/05/11	11/14/11	11/16/11	12/16/11
.075	02/01/12	02/27/12	02/29/12	03/30/12

COVIDIEN PLC

Symbol: COV (NYSE)
Price: $51.50 (as of 01/31/12)
Ratings:
   The Street: BUY
   Standard & Poor's: STRONG BUY ★ ★ ★ ★ ★
   Ford Equity Research: BUY
Sector: Health Care
Industry: Medical Instruments and Supplies
52-Week Range: $41.35 (10/04/11)-Low
                 $57.65 (05/19/11)-High
Shares Outstanding: 482.43M
Beta: .77
P/E (Trailing 12-Month): $13.14
EPS (Trailing 12-Month): $3.92
Annual Dividend per Share and Yield: $.90/1.70%
Market Capitalization: $24.84B
Founded: 2000
Employees: 41,300
Website: http://www.covidien.com
Address: (Principal Executive Office)
Covidien Plc
20 On Hatch
Lower Hatch Street
Dublin 2, Ireland
Phone: +353 (1) 438-1700
Address: (U.S.)
Covidien
15 Hampshire Street
Mansfield, MA 02048
Phone: (508) 261-8000
Investor Relations:
Phone: (508) 452-4650
Email: Investor.Relations@covidien.com
Company Summary: Covidien PLC, formerly Tyco Health Care, engages in the manufacture and distribution of medical devices and supplies.

Revenue (Millions $)

Year	1st Q	2nd Q	3rd Q	4th Q	Year Total
2008:	2,316	2,426	2,595	2,573	9,910
2009:	2,564	2,798	2,618	2,697	10,677
2010:	2,644	2,551	2,564	2,670	10,429
2011:	2,769	2,801	2,926	3,078	11,574
2012:	2,898	—	—	—	—

Dividends (per share-last four)

$	Date Declared	Ex-Dividend Date	Date of Record	Payment Date
.20	03/15/11	04/05/11	04/07/11	05/06/11
.20	07/20/11	07/28/11	08/01/11	08/19/11
.225	09/22/11	10/11/11	10/13/11	11/04/11
.225	01/19/12	01/26/12	01/30/12	02/22/12

CUMMINS, INC.

Symbol: CMI (NYSE)
Price: $104.00 (as of 01/31/12)
Ratings:
   The Street: BUY
   Standard & Poor's: STRONG BUY ★ ★ ★ ★ ★
   Ford Equity Research: BUY
Sector: Industrials
Industry: Diversified Machinery
52-Week Range: $79.53 (10/04/11)-Low
                 $110.95 (01/26/12)-High
Shares Outstanding: 190.20M
Beta: 1.76
P/E (Trailing 12-Month): $12.18
EPS (Trailing 12-Month): $8.54
Annual Dividend per Share and Yield: $1.60/1.50%
Market Capitalization: $19.86B
Founded: 1919
Employees: 43,900
Website: http://www.cummins.com
Address: (U.S.)
Cummins, Inc.
500 Jackson Street
PO Box 3005
Columbus, IN 47202-3005
Phone: (812) 377-5000
Investor Relations:
Phone: (812) 377-3121
E-mail: mark.a.smith@cummins.com
Company Summary: Cummins, Inc. designs, manufactures, distributes and services engines and related technologies, which includes fuel systems, controls, air handling, filtration, emission control and electrical power generation systems.

Revenue (Millions $)

Year	1st Q	2nd Q	3rd Q	4th Q	Year Total
2008:	3,474	3,887	3,693	3,288	14,342
2009:	2,439	2,431	2,530	3,400	10,800
2010:	2,478	3,208	3,401	4,139	13,226
2011:	3,860	4,641	4,626	4,921	18,048

Dividends (per share-last four)

$	Date Declared	Ex-Dividend Date	Date of Record	Payment Date
.2625	05/10/11	05/18/11	05/20/11	06/01/11
.40	07/12/11	08/18/11	08/22/11	09/01/11
.40	10/16/11	11/17/11	11/21/11	12/01/11
.40	02/14/12	02/22/12	02/24/12	03/01/12

CVS CAREMARK CORP.

Symbol: CVS (NYSE)
Price: $41.75 (as of 01/31/12)
Ratings:
   The Street: BUY
   Standard & Poor's: STRONG BUY ★ ★ ★ ★ ★
   Ford Equity Research: BUY
Sector: Consumer Services
Industry: Drug Retail
52-Week Range: $31.30 (08/09/11)-Low
                 $43.17 (01/19/12)-High
Shares Outstanding: 1.30B
Beta: .82
P/E (Trailing 12-Month): $16.65
EPS (Trailing 12-Month): $2.51
Annual Dividend per Share and Yield: $.65/1.50%
Market Capitalization: $54.34B
Founded: 2007 (by merger of CVS Corp. and Caremark Rx, Inc.)
Employees: 200,000
Website: http://www.info.cvscaremark.com
Address: (U.S.)
CVS Caremark Corp.
One CVS Drive
Woonsocket, RI 02895
Phone: (401) 765-1500
Investor Relations:
E-mail: investorinfo@cvs.com
Company Summary: CVS Caremark Corp. is a drug retail company that operates a chain of U.S. pharmacies. The company also offers mail order and online services to its customers.

Revenue (Millions $)

Year	1st Q	2nd Q	3rd Q	4th Q	Year Total
2008:	21,326	21,140	20,863	24,142	87,472
2009:	23,394	24,871	24,642	25,822	98,729
2010:	23,760	24,007	23,875	24,771	96,413
2011:	25,880	26,629	26,274	28,317	107,100

Dividends (per share-last four)

$	Date Declared	Ex-Dividend Date	Date of Record	Payment Date
.125	07/06/11	07/20/11	07/22/11	08/02/11
.125	09/21/11	10/19/11	10/21/11	11/01/11
.1625	12/20/11	01/19/12	01/23/12	02/02/12
.1625	03/07/12	04/19/12	04/23/12	05/03/12

DAVITA, INC.

Symbol: DVA (NYSE)
Price: $81.81 (as of 01/31/12)
Ratings:
    The Street: BUY
    Standard & Poor's: BUY ★ ★ ★ ★
    Ford Equity Research: BUY
Sector: Health Care
Industry: Specialized Health Care Services
52-Week Range: $59.14 (10/04/11)-Low
                      $89.76 (07/07/11)-High
Shares Outstanding: 93.70M
Beta: .38
P/E (Trailing 12-Month): $19.93
EPS (Trailing 12-Month): $4.10
Annual Dividend per Share and Yield: N/A
Market Capitalization: $7.65B
Founded: 1999
Employees: 36,500
Website: http://www.davita.com
Address: (U.S.)
DaVita, Inc.
1551 Wewatta Street
Denver, CO 80202
Phone: (303) 405-2100
Investor Relations:
E-mail: ir@davita.com
Company Summary: DaVita, Inc. engages in renal care and specializes in hemodialysis, peritoneal dialysis, home hemodialysis, vascular access management, chronic kidney disease education, and renal diet assistance.

Revenue (Millions $)

Year	1st Q	2nd Q	3rd Q	4th Q	Year Total
2008:	1,345	1,407	1,447	1,461	5,660
2009:	1,448	1,519	1,574	1,568	6,109
2010:	1,559	1,587	1,652	1,649	6,447
2011:	1,606	1,712	1,808	1,862	6,988

Dividends (none)

DELL, INC.
Symbol: DELL (NASDAQ)
Price: $17.23 (as of 01/31/12)
Ratings:
> **The Street:** BUY
> **Standard & Poor's:** BUY ★ ★ ★ ★
> **Ford Equity Research:** BUY

Sector: Information Technology
Industry: Personal Computers
52-Week Range: $13.29 (08/18/11)-Low
$17.23 (01/31/11)-High
Shares Outstanding: 1.76B
Beta: 1.26
P/E (Trailing 12-Month): $8.87
EPS (Trailing 12-Month): $1.94
Annual Dividend per Share and Yield: N/A
Market Capitalization: $30.95B
Founded: 1984
Employees: 103,300
Website: http://www.dell.com
Address: (U.S.)
Dell, Inc.
One Dell Way
Round Rock, TX 78682
Phone: (512) 338-4400
Investor Relations:
E-mail: investor_relations_fulfillment@dell.com
Company Summary: Dell, Inc. is a computer technology corporation that develops, sells and supports computers and related products and services.

Dell, Inc. (DELL)

Revenue (Millions $)

Year	1st Q	2nd Q	3rd Q	4th Q	Year Total
2008:	14,722	14,776	15,646	15,989	61,133
2009:	16,077	16,434	15,162	13,428	61,101
2010:	12,342	12,764	12,896	14,900	52,902
2011:	14,874	15,534	15,394	15,692	61,494
2012:	15,017	15,658	15,365	16,031	62,071

Dividends (none)

DISCOVER FINANCIAL SERVICES, INC.

Symbol: DFS (NYSE)
Price: $27.18 (as of 01/31/12)
Ratings:

   The Street: BUY
   Standard & Poor's: BUY ★ ★ ★ ★
   Ford Equity Research: STRONG BUY
Sector: Financials
Industry: Consumer Credit Services
52-Week Range: $20.51 (08/08/11)-Low
                  $28.09 (01/26/12)-High
Shares Outstanding: 529.98M
Beta: 1.54
P/E (Trailing 12-Month): $6.69
EPS (Trailing 12-Month): $4.06
Annual Dividend per Share and Yield: $.40/1.50%
Market Capitalization: $14.40B
Founded: 1985
Employees: 11,650
Website: http://www.discoverfinancial.com
Address: (U.S.)
Discover Financial Services, Inc.
2500 Lake Cook Road
Riverwoods, IL 60015
Phone: (224) 405-0900
Investor Relations:
Phone: (224) 405-4555
E-mail: investorrelations@discover.com
Company Summary: Discover Financial Services, Inc. is a financial services company, which issues the Discover Card and operates the Discover and Pulse networks.

Revenue (Millions $)

Year	1st Q	2nd Q	3rd Q	4th Q	Year Total
2008:	1,638	1,457	1,557	2,305	6,957
2009:	2,006	1,939	2,149	1,892	7,986
2010:	2,105	2,065	2,100	1,971	8,241
2011:	2,116	2,117	2,151	2,166	8,550

Dividends (per share-last four)

$	Date Declared	Ex-Dividend Date	Date of Record	Payment Date
.06	06/14/11	07/05/11	07/07/11	07/21/11
.06	09/14/11	10/04/11	10/06/11	10/20/11
.10	12/15/11	12/27/11	12/29/11	01/19/12
.10	03/13/12	04/03/12	04/05/12	04/19/12

DOW CHEMICAL CO.

Symbol: DOW (NYSE)
Price: $33.51 (as of 01/31/12)
Ratings:
  The Street: BUY
  Standard & Poor's: HOLD ★ ★ ★ ☆ ☆
  Ford Equity Research: HOLD
Sector: Materials
Industry: Chemical Products
52-Week Range: $20.61 (10/04/11)-Low
            $42.23 (05/02/11)-High
Shares Outstanding: 1.19B
Beta: 3.0
P/E (Trailing 12-Month): $13.72
EPS (Trailing 12-Month): $2.44
Annual Dividend per Share and Yield: $1.00/3.00%
Market Capitalization: $39.60B
Founded: 1897
Employees: 51,705
Website: http://www.dow.com
Address: (U.S.)
The Dow Chemical Co.
2030 Dow Center
Midland, MI 48674
Phone: (989) 636-1000
Investor Relations:
Phone: (800) 422-8193
Company Summary: The Dow Chemical Co. ranks as the as one of the largest chemical manufacturers in the world. The company is a provider of plastics, chemicals, and agricultural products in approximately 160 countries.

Revenue (Millions $)

Year	1st Q	2nd Q	3rd Q	4th Q	Year Total
2008:	14,824	16,380	15,411	10,899	57,514
2009:	9,041	11,322	12,046	12,466	44,875
2010:	13,417	13,618	12,868	13,771	53,674
2011:	14,733	16,046	15,109	14,097	59,985

Dividends (per share-last four)

$	Date Declared	Ex-Dividend Date	Date of Record	Payment Date
.25	04/14/11	06/28/11	06/30/11	07/29/11
.25	09/15/11	09/28/11	09/30/11	10/28/11
.25	12/15/11	12/28/11	12/30/11	01/30/12
.25	02/09/12	03/28/12	03/30/12	04/30/12

DR. PEPPER SNAPPLE GROUP, INC.

Symbol: DPS (NYSE)
Price: $38.82 (as of 01/31/12)
Ratings:
    The Street: BUY
    Standard & Poor's: HOLD ★ ★ ★
    Ford Equity Research: BUY
Sector: Consumer Goods
Industry: Beverages
52-Week Range: $34.37 (08/09/11)-Low
                         $43.13 (07/05/11)-High
Shares Outstanding: 212.07M
Beta: .54
P/E (Trailing 12-Month): $15.79
EPS (Trailing 12-Month): $2.46
Annual Dividend per Share and Yield: $1.28/3.30%
Market Capitalization: $8.32B
Founded: 2007
Employees: 19,000
Website: http://www.drpeppersnapple.com
Address: (U.S.)
Dr Pepper Snapple Group, Inc.
5301 Legacy Drive
Plano, TX 75024
Phone: (972) 673-7000
Investor Relations:
Phone: (972) 673-7935
Company Summary: Dr Pepper Snapple Group, Inc. is a beverage company that produces the following key brands: 7UP, A&W, Cactus Cooler, Canada Dry, Clamato, Coco Casa, Country Time, Crush, Deja Blue, Diet Rite, Dr Pepper, Elements, Hawaiian Punch, Hires, Holland House, IBC, Margaritaville, Mistic, Mott's, Mr & Mrs T, Nantucket Nectars, Nehi, Orangina, Peñafiel, RC Cola, ReaLemon, Rose's, Schweppes, Snapple, Squirt, Stewart's, Sun Drop, Sunkist, Tahitian Treat, Venom Energy, Vernors, Welch's and Yoo-hoo.

Revenue (Millions $)

Year	1st Q	2nd Q	3rd Q	4th Q	Year Total
2008:	1,295	1,545	1,494	1,376	5,710
2009:	1,260	1,481	1,434	1,356	5,531
2010:	1,248	1,519	1,457	1,412	5,636
2011:	1,331	1,582	1,529	1,461	5,903

Dividends (per share-last four)

$	Date Declared	Ex-Dividend Date	Date of Record	Payment Date
.32	05/18/11	06/16/11	06/20/11	07/08/11
.32	08/11/11	09/15/11	09/19/11	10/07/11
.32	11/17/11	12/15/11	12/19/11	01/06/12
.34	02/08/12	03/15/12	03/19/12	04/06/12

E. I. DU PONT DE NEMOURS AND CO.

Symbol: DD (NYSE)
Price: $50.89 (as of 01/31/12)
Ratings:
    The Street: BUY
    Standard & Poor's: BUY ★ ★ ★ ★
    Ford Equity Research: HOLD
Sector: Materials
Industry: Diversified Chemicals
52-Week Range: $37.10 (10/04/11)-Low
                 $57.00 (05/02/11)-High
Shares Outstanding: 932.25M
Beta: 1.62
P/E (Trailing 12-Month): $13.83
EPS (Trailing 12-Month): $3.68
Annual Dividend per Share and Yield: $1.64/3.20%
Market Capitalization: $47.13B
Founded: 1802
Employees: 70,000
Website: http://www.dupont.com
Address: (U.S.)
E. I. du Pont de Nemours and Co.
1007 Market Street
Wilmington, DE 19898
Phone: (302) 774-1000
Investor Relations:
Phone: (302) 774-3034
Company Summary: E. I. du Pont de Nemours and Co., commonly referred to as DuPont, is a chemical company that has developed many polymers such as Vespel, neoprene, nylon, Corian, Teflon, Mylar, Kevlar, Zemdrain, M5 fiber, Nomex, Tyvek, Sorona and Lycra. The company ranks as the world's third largest chemical company based on market capitalization.

Revenue (Millions $)

Year	1st Q	2nd Q	3rd Q	4th Q	Year Total
2008:	8,575	8,837	7,297	5,820	30,529
2009:	6,871	6,858	5,961	6,419	26,109
2010:	8,484	8,616	7,067	7,404	31,571
2011:	10,059	10,493	9,399	8,425	38,376

Dividends (per share-last four)

$	Date Declared	Ex-Dividend Date	Date of Record	Payment Date
.41	04/27/11	05/11/11	05/13/11	06/10/11
.41	07/15/11	08/11/11	08/15/11	09/12/11
.41	10/20/11	11/10/11	11/15/11	12/14/11
.41	01/24/12	02/13/12	02/15/12	03/14/12

EASTMAN CHEMICAL CO.

Symbol: EMN (NYSE)
Price: $50.32 (as of 01/31/12)
Ratings:
   The Street: BUY
   Standard & Poor's: BUY ★ ★ ★ ★
   Ford Equity Research: HOLD
Sector: Materials
Industry: Diversified Chemicals
52-Week Range: $32.45 (09/22/11)-Low
                   $55.36 (04/29/11)-High
Shares Outstanding: 136.92M
Beta: 2.25
P/E (Trailing 12-Month): $10.35
EPS (Trailing 12-Month): $4.86
Annual Dividend per Share and Yield: $1.04/2.10%
Market Capitalization: $6.89B
Founded: 1920
Employees: 10,000
Website: http://www.eastman.com
Address: (U.S.)
Eastman Chemical Co.
200 South Wilcox Drive
Kingsport, TN 37662
Phone: (423) 229-2000
Investor Relations:
Phone: (212) 835-1620
E-mail: griddle@eastman.com
Company Summary: Eastman Chemical Co. is a company engaged in the manufacture and sale of chemicals, fibers, and plastics.

Revenue (Millions $)

Year	1st Q	2nd Q	3rd Q	4th Q	Year Total
2008:	1,727	1,834	1,819	1,346	6,726
2009:	1,129	1,253	1,337	1,328	5,047
2010:	1,370	1,502	1,507	1,463	5,842
2011:	1,758	1,885	1,812	1,723	7,178

Dividends (per share-last four)

$	Date Declared	Ex-Dividend Date	Date of Record	Payment Date
.47	05/05/11	06/13/11	06/15/11	07/01/11
.52	08/05/11	09/13/11	09/15/11	10/03/11
.26	12/01/11	12/13/11	12/15/11	01/03/12
.26	02/16/12	03/13/12	03/15/12	04/02/12

EOG RESOURCES, INC.

Symbol: EOG (NYSE)
Price: $106.14 (as of 01/31/12)
Ratings:
  The Street: BUY
  Standard & Poor's: BUY ★ ★ ★ ★
  Ford Equity Research: HOLD
Sector: Energy
Industry: Oil and Gas Production
52-Week Range: $66.81 (10/04/11)-Low
                   $121.44 (03/30/11)-High
Shares Outstanding: 269.08M
Beta: 1.45
P/E (Trailing 12-Month): $27.22
EPS (Trailing 12-Month): $3.90
Annual Dividend per Share and Yield: $.64/.60%
Market Capitalization: $28.54B
Founded: 1999
Employees: 2,550
Website: http://www.eogresources.com
Address: (U.S.)
EOG Resources, Inc.
1111 Bagby
Sky Lobby 2
Houston, TX 77002
Phone: (713) 651-7000
Investor Relations:
Phone: (877) 363-3647
E-mail: IR@eogresources.com
Company Summary: EOG Resources, Inc. is one of the largest independent oil and natural gas companies in the United States.

Revenue (Millions $)

Year	1st Q	2nd Q	3rd Q	4th Q	Year Total
2008:	1,101	1,033	3,220	1,773	7,127
2009:	1,158	861	1,007	1,761	4,787
2010:	1,371	1,358	1,582	1,789	6,100
2011:	1,897	2,570	2,886	2,773	10,126

Dividends (per share-last four)

$	Date Declared	Ex-Dividend Date	Date of Record	Payment Date
.16	05/04/11	07/13/11	07/15/11	07/29/11
.16	09/07/11	10/13/11	10/17/11	10/31/11
.16	12/16/11	01/12/12	01/17/11	01/31/12
.17	02/16/12	04/12/12	04/16/12	04/30/12

FASTENAL CO.

Symbol: FAST (NASDAQ)
Price: $46.68 (as of 01/31/12)
Ratings:
   The Street: BUY
   Standard & Poor's: STRONG BUY ★ ★ ★ ★ ★
   Ford Equity Research: BUY
Sector: Industrials
Industry: Materials Distributors
52-Week Range: $29.14 (08/09/11)-Low
                  $47.18 (01/26/12)-High
Shares Outstanding: 295.28M
Beta: .91
P/E (Trailing 12-Month): $38.58
EPS (Trailing 12-Month): $1.51
Annual Dividend per Share and Yield: $.68/1.50%
Market Capitalization: $13.78B
Founded: 1967
Employees: 15,168
Website: http://www.fastenal.com
Address: (U.S.)
Fastenal Co.
2001 Theurer Boulevard
Winona, MN 55987-0978
Phone: (507) 454-5374
Investor Relations:
Phone: (507) 454-5374
Company Summary: Fastenal Co. distributes industrial and construction supplies and offers services including inventory management, manufacturing and tool repair.

Revenue (Millions $)

Year	1st Q	2nd Q	3rd Q	4th Q	Year Total
2008:	566	604	625	545	2,340
2009:	489	475	489	477	1,930
2010:	521	571	604	574	2,270
2011:	641	702	727	698	2,768

Dividends (per share-last four)

$	Date Declared	Ex-Dividend Date	Date of Record	Payment Date
.13	04/11/11	04/13/11	04/12/11	04/28/11
.13	07/11/11	07/21/11	07/25/11	08/22/11
.14	10/12/11	10/24/11	10/26/11	11/22/11
.17	01/17/12	01/30/12	02/01/12	02/29/12

FEDEX CORP.

Symbol: FDX (NYSE)
Price: $91.49 (as of 01/31/12)
Ratings:
   The Street: BUY
   Standard & Poor's: STRONG BUY ★ ★ ★ ★ ★
   Ford Equity Research: BUY
Sector: Industrials
Industry: Logistics and Air Freight
52-Week Range: $64.07 (10/04/11)-Low
                   $98.66 (07/07/11)-High
Shares Outstanding: 314.48M
Beta: 1.66
P/E (Trailing 12-Month): $16.64
EPS (Trailing 12-Month): $5.50
Annual Dividend per Share and Yield: $.52/.60%
Market Capitalization: $28.77B
Founded: 1971
Employees: 290,000
Website: http://www.fedex.com
Address: (U.S.)
FedEx Corp.
942 South Shady Grove Road
Memphis, TN 38120
Phone: (901) 818-7500
Investor Relations:
Phone: (901) 818-7500
Company Summary: FedEx Corp. is a logistics services
company specializing in package and heavy freight delivery.

Revenue (Millions $)

Year	1st Q	2nd. Q	3rd Q	4th Q	Year Total
2008:	9,199	9,451	9,437	9,866	37,953
2009:	9,970	9,538	8,137	7,852	35,497
2010:	8,009	8,596	8,701	9,428	34,734
2011:	9,457	9,632	9,663	10,552	39,304
2012:	10,521	10,587	—	—	—

Dividends (per share-last four)

$	Date Declared	Ex-Dividend Date	Date of Record	Payment Date
.13	06/06/11	06/15/11	06/17/11	07/01/11
.13	08/19/11	09/08/11	09/12/11	10/03/11
.13	11/18/11	12/09/11	12/13/11	01/03/12
.13	02/17/12	03/08/12	03/12/12	04/02/12

FLOWSERVE CORP.

Symbol: FLS (NYSE)
Price: $110.17 (as of 01/31/12)
Ratings:
    The Street: BUY
    Standard & Poor's: STRONG BUY ★ ★ ★ ★ ★
    Ford Equity Research: HOLD
Sector: Industrials
Industry: Industrial Supplies
52-Week Range: $66.84 (10/04/11)-Low
                  $135.72 (04/26/11)-High
Shares Outstanding: 54.50M
Beta: 1.6
P/E (Trailing 12-Month): $14.91
EPS (Trailing 12-Month): $7.39
Annual Dividend per Share and Yield: $1.28/1.20%
Market Capitalization: $6.12B
Founded: 1997 (by merger of BW/IP International, Inc. and Durco International)
Employees: 15,000
Website: http://www.flowserve.com
Address: (U.S.)
Flowserve Corp.
5215 North O'Connor Boulevard
Suite 2300
Irving, TX 75039
Phone: (972) 443-6500
Investor Relations:
Phone: (972) 443-6500
Company Summary: The Flowserve Corp. is a supplier of pumps, valves, seals, automation and services to the power, oil and gas, and chemical industries.

Revenue (Millions $)

Year	1st Q	2nd Q	3rd Q	4th Q	Year Total
2008:	993	1,158	1,154	1,169	4,473
2009:	1,025	1,090	1,051	1,199	4,365
2010:	959	961	972	1,140	4,032
2011:	997	1,126	1,122	1,265	4,510

Dividends (per share-last four)

$	Date Declared	Ex-Dividend Date	Date of Record	Payment Date
.32	05/19/11	06/28/11	06/30/11	07/14/11
.32	08/12/11	09/28/11	09/30/11	10/14/11
.32	11/18/11	12/28/11	12/30/11	01/13/12
.36	02/21/12	03/28/12	03/30/12	04/13/12

FORD MOTOR CO.

Symbol: F (NYSE)
Price: $12.42 (as of 01/31/12)
Ratings:
    The Street: BUY
    Standard & Poor's: BUY ★ ★ ★ ★
    Ford Equity Research: HOLD
Sector: Consumer Goods
Industry: Automobile Manufacturers
52-Week Range: $9.05 (10/04/11)-Low
                 $16.18 (04/26/11)-High
Shares Outstanding: 3.80B
Beta: 2.53
P/E (Trailing 12-Month): $7.45
EPS (Trailing 12-Month): $1.67
Annual Dividend per Share and Yield: $.20/1.60%
Market Capitalization: $47.20B
Founded: 1903
Employees: 164,000
Website: http://www.ford.com
Address: (U.S.)
Ford Motor Co.
One American Road
Dearborn, MI 48126
Phone: (313) 322-3000
Investor Relations:
Phone: (800) 555-5259

Company Summary: Ford Motor Co. is an automaker that produces the Ford and Lincoln brands. The company ranks as the world's third largest manufacturer of cars and trucks and also owns a stake in Mazda in Japan and Aston Martin in the United Kingdom.

Revenue (Millions $)

Year	1st Q	2nd Q	3rd Q	4th Q	Year Total
2008:	43,513	38,600	32,100	29,200	143,413
2009:	24,778	27,189	30,892	35,449	118,308
2010:	31,566	31,300	29,893	32,428	125,187
2011:	33,114	35,527	33,047	34,576	136,264

Dividends (per share-last four)

$	Date Declared	Ex-Dividend Date	Date of Record	Payment Date
.10	03/08/06	04/28/06	05/02/06	06/01/06
.05	07/13/06	07/31/06	08/02/06	09/01/06
.05	12/08/11	01/27/12	01/31/12	03/01/12
.05	03/14/12	04/30/12	05/02/12	06/01/12

GENERAL MILLS, INC.

Symbol: GIS (NYSE)
Price: $39.83 (as of 01/31/12)
Ratings:
   The Street: BUY
   Standard & Poor's: STRONG BUY ★ ★ ★ ★
   Ford Equity Research: HOLD
Sector: Consumer Goods
Industry: Processed Foods
52-Week Range: $34.64 (08/09/11)-Low
                   $41.06 (01/17/12)-High
Shares Outstanding: 644.65M
Beta: .16
P/E (Trailing 12-Month): $16.96
EPS (Trailing 12-Month): $2.35
Annual Dividend per Share and Yield: $1.22/3.00%
Market Capitalization: $25.68B
Founded: 1928
Employees: 35,000
Website: http://www.generalmills.com
Address: (U.S.)
General Mills, Inc.
Number One General Mills Boulevard
Minneapolis, MN 55426
Phone: (763) 764-7600
Investor Relations:
Phone: (800) 245-5703
Company Summary: General Mills, Inc. is a producer of food products, which includes brands such as Betty Crocker, Yoplait, Colombo, Totinos, Jeno's, Pillsbury, Green Giant, Old El Paso, Häagen-Dazs, Cheerios, Lucky Charms and Wanchai Ferry.

Revenue (Millions $)

Year	1st Q	2nd Q	3rd Q	4th Q	Year Total
2008:	3,072	3,703	3,406	3,471	13,652
2009:	3,497	4,011	3,537	3,646	14,691
2010:	3,519	4,078	3,629	3,570	14,797
2011:	3,533	4,067	3,646	3,634	14,880
2012:	3,848	4,624	—	—	—

Dividends (per share-last four)

$	Date Declared	Ex-Dividend Date	Date of Record	Payment Date
.305	06/28/11	07/07/11	07/11/11	08/01/11
.305	09/26/11	10/05/11	10/10/11	11/01/11
.305	12/13/11	01/06/12	01/10/12	02/01/12
.305	03/13/12	04/05/12	04/10/12	05/01/12

GOODYEAR TIRE & RUBBER CO.

Symbol: GT (NYSE)
Price: $13.00 (as of 01/31/12)
Ratings:
>   **The Street:** HOLD
>   **Standard & Poor's:** HOLD ★ ★ ★
>   **Ford Equity Research:** HOLD

Sector: Consumer Goods
Industry: Tires and Rubber
52-Week Range: $8.53 (10/04/11)-Low
> $18.83 (05/10/11)-High

Shares Outstanding: 244.56M
Beta: 2.96
P/E (Trailing 12-Month): $24.12
EPS (Trailing 12-Month): $.54
Annual Dividend per Share and Yield: N/A
Market Capitalization: $3.18B
Founded: 1898
Employees: 73,000
Website: http://www.goodyear.com
Address: (U.S.)
Goodyear Tire & Rubber Co.
1144 East Market Street
Akron, OH 44316-0001
Phone: (330) 796-2121
Investor Relations:
E-mail: goodyear.investor.relations@goodyear.com
Company Summary: The Goodyear Tire & Rubber Co. manufactures tires for automobiles, commercial trucks, light trucks, SUVs, race cars, airplanes, farm equipment and heavy earth-mover machinery.

Revenue (Millions $)

Year	1st Q	2nd Q	3rd Q	4th Q	Year Total
2008:	4,942	5,239	5,172	4,135	19,488
2009:	3,536	3,943	4,385	4,437	16,301
2010:	4,270	4,528	4,962	5,072	18,832
2011:	5,402	5,620	6,062	5,683	22,767

Dividends (last paid in 2002)

W. W. GRAINGER, INC.

Symbol: GWW (NYSE)
Price: $190.74 (as of 01/31/12)
Ratings:
  The Street: BUY
  Standard & Poor's: BUY ★ ★ ★ ★
  Ford Equity Research: BUY
Sector: Industrials
Industry: Industrial Equipment Distributors
52-Week Range: $124.33 (08/09/11)-Low
              $204.62 (01/24/12)-High
Shares Outstanding: 70.10M
Beta: .91
P/E (Trailing 12-Month): $21.02
EPS (Trailing 12-Month): $9.07
Annual Dividend per Share and Yield: $2.64/1.40%
Market Capitalization: $13.34B
Founded: 1927
Employees: 20,000
Website: http://www.grainger.com
Address: (U.S.)
W. W. Grainger, Inc.
100 Grainger Parkway
Lake Forest, IL 60045-5201
Phone: (847) 535-1000
Investor Relations:
Phone: (847) 535-0881
Email: william.chapman@grainger.com
Company Summary: W. W. Grainger, Inc. is an industrial supply company offering such products as motors, lighting, material handling, fasteners, plumbing, tools, and safety supplies.

Revenue (Millions $)

Year	1st Q	2nd Q	3rd Q	4th Q	Year Total
2008:	1,661	1,757	1,839	1,593	6,850
2009:	1,465	1,533	1,590	1,634	6,222
2010:	1,672	1,784	1,899	1,827	7,182
2011:	1,884	2,003	2,115	2,077	8,079

Dividends (per share-last four)

$	Date Declared	Ex-Dividend Date	Date of Record	Payment Date
.66	04/27/11	05/05/11	05/09/11	06/01/11
.66	07/27/11	08/04/11	08/08/11	09/01/11
.66	10/26/11	11/09/11	11/14/11	12/01/11
.66	01/25/12	02/09/12	02/13/12	03/01/12

HALLIBURTON CO.

Symbol: HAL (NYSE)
Price: $36.78 (as of 01/31/12)
Ratings:
   The Street: BUY
   Standard & Poor's: BUY ★ ★ ★ ★
   Ford Equity Research: HOLD
Sector: Energy
Industry: Oil and Gas Equipment and Services
52-Week Range: $27.21 (10/04/11)-Low
                   $57.77 (07/25/11)-High
Shares Outstanding: 922.98M
Beta: 1.5
P/E (Trailing 12-Month): $11.94
EPS (Trailing 12-Month): $3.08
Annual Dividend per Share and Yield: $.36/1.00%
Market Capitalization: $33.87B
Founded: 1919
Employees: 68,000
Website: http://www.halliburton.com
Address: (U.S.)
Halliburton Co.
3000 North Sam Houston Parkway East
Houston, TX 77032
Phone: (281) 871-2699
Investor Relations:
Phone: (888) 669-3920
E-mail: investors@halliburton.com
Company Summary: Halliburton Co. is an oilfield services companies that provides products and services to the oil and gas industry.

Revenue (Millions $)

Year	1st Q	2nd Q	3rd Q	4th Q	Year Total
2008:	4,029	4,487	4,853	4,910	18,279
2009:	3,907	3,494	3,588	3,686	14,675
2010:	3,761	4,387	4,665	5,160	17,973
2011:	5,282	5,935	6,548	7,064	24,829

Dividends (per share-last four)

$	Date Declared	Ex-Dividend Date	Date of Record	Payment Date
.09	05/19/11	05/27/11	06/01/11	06/22/11
.09	07/22/11	08/30/11	09/01/11	09/22/11
.09	11/07/11	11/30/11	12/02/11	12/23/11
.09	02/16/12	03/05/12	03/07/12	03/28/12

HARRIS CORP.

Symbol: HRS (NYSE)
Price: $41.00 (as of 01/31/12)
Ratings:
   The Street: BUY
   Standard & Poor's: STRONG BUY ★ ★ ★ ★ ★
   Ford Equity Research: BUY
Sector: Information Technology
Industry: Communication Equipment
52-Week Range: $32.68 (10/04/11)-Low
$53.39 (05/02/11)-High
Shares Outstanding: 113.87M
Beta: .72
P/E (Trailing 12-Month): $9.44
EPS (Trailing 12-Month): $4.34
Annual Dividend per Share and Yield: $1.12/2.80%
Market Capitalization: $4.75B
Founded: 1895 (as the Harris Automatic Press Company)
Employees: 16,900
Website: http://www.harris.com
Address: (U.S.)
Harris Corp.
1025 West NASA Boulevard
Melbourne, FL 32919-0001
Phone: (321) 727-9100
Investor Relations:
Phone: (321) 724-3231
E-mail: jfronk@harris.com
Company Summary: Harris Corp. is a communications equipment company that produces wireless equipment, electronic systems, and both terrestrial and space borne antennas for use in the government, defense, and commercial sectors.

Revenue (Millions $)

Year	1st Q	2nd Q	3rd Q	4th Q	Year Total
2008:	1,231	1,318	1,330	1,433	5,311
2009:	1,173	1,333	1,205	1,294	5,005
2010:	1,203	1,218	1,330	1,456	5,206
2011:	1,405	1,439	1,413	1,667	5,925
2012:	1,460	1,446	—	—	—

Dividends (per share-last four)

$	Date Declared	Ex-Dividend Date	Date of Record	Payment Date
.25	04/21/11	05/26/11	05/31/11	06/10/11
.28	07/30/11	09/02/11	09/07/11	09/16/11
.28	10/28/11	11/16/11	11/18/11	12/02/11
.33	02/24/12	03/05/12	03/07/12	03/16/12

INTERNATIONAL BUSINESS MACHINES CORP.

Symbol: IBM (NYSE)
Price: $192.60 (as of 01/31/12)
Ratings:
    The Street: BUY
    Standard & Poor's: STRONG BUY ★ ★ ★ ★
    Ford Equity Research: STRONG BUY
Sector: Information Technology
Industry: IT Consulting and Computer Services
52-Week Range: $157.13 (08/19/11)-Low
                      $193.10 (01/31/12)-High
Shares Outstanding: 1.16B
Beta: .41
P/E (Trailing 12-Month): $14.75
EPS (Trailing 12-Month): $13.06
Annual Dividend per Share and Yield: $3.00/1.60%
Market Capitalization: $223.42B
Founded: 1911
Employees: 440,885
Website: http://www.ibm.com
Address: (U.S.)
International Business Machines Corp.
1 New Orchard Road
Armonk, NY 10504-1722
Phone: (914) 499-1900
Investor Relations:
Phone: (914) 499-1900
Company Summary: International Business Machines Corp. is a technology and consulting corporation that manufactures and sells computer hardware and software, and also offers infrastructure, hosting and consulting services in areas ranging from mainframe computers to nanotechnology.

Revenue (Millions $)

Year	1st Q	2nd Q	3rd Q	4th Q	Year Total
2008:	24,502	26,820	25,302	27,006	103,630
2009:	21,711	23,251	23,565	27,232	95,759
2010:	22,857	23,724	24,271	29,019	99,871
2011:	24,607	26,666	26,157	29,486	106,916

Dividends (per share-last four)

$	Date Declared	Ex-Dividend Date	Date of Record	Payment Date
.75	04/24/11	05/06/11	05/10/11	06/10/11
.75	07/26/11	08/08/11	08/10/11	09/10/11
.75	10/25/11	11/08/11	11/10/11	12/10/11
.75	01/31/12	02/08/12	02/10/12	03/10/12

INTERPUBLIC GROUP OF COMPANIES, INC.

Symbol: IPG (NYSE)
Price: $10.33 (as of 01/31/12)
Ratings:
The Street: BUY
Standard & Poor's: BUY ★ ★ ★ ★
Ford Equity Research: BUY
Sector: Consumer Services
Industry: Advertising
52-Week Range: $6.73 (10/04/11)-Low
$12.91 (07/07/11)-High
Shares Outstanding: 446.11M
Beta: 1.79
P/E (Trailing 12-Month): $12.07
EPS (Trailing 12-Month): $.86
Annual Dividend per Share and Yield: $.24/2.40%
Market Capitalization: $4.76B
Founded: 1902
Employees: 42,000
Website: http://www.interpublic.com
Address: (U.S.)
The Interpublic Group of Companies, Inc.
1114 Avenue of the Americas
New York, NY 10036
Phone: (212) 704-1200
Investor Relations:
Phone: (212) 704-1200
Company Summary: The Interpublic Group of Companies, Inc. is an advertising holding company with subsidiaries specializing in consumer advertising, interactive marketing, media planning and buying, public relations, and sports and event marketing.

Revenue (Millions $)

Year	1st Q	2nd Q	3rd Q	4th Q	Year Total
2008:	1,485	1,835	1,740	1,902	6,962
2009:	1,325	1,474	1,426	1,781	6,007
2010:	1,337	1,611	1,553	2,005	6,507
2011:	1,475	1,741	1,726	2,072	7,014

Dividends (per share-last four)

$	Date Declared	Ex-Dividend Date	Date of Record	Payment Date
.06	05/26/11	06/08/11	06/10/11	06/24/11
.06	07/28/11	09/07/11	09/09/11	09/23/11
.06	10/27/11	11/29/11	12/01/11	12/15/11
.06	02/23/12	03/07/12	03/09/12	03/23/12

JACOBS ENGINEERING GROUP, INC.

Symbol: JEC (NYSE)
Price: $44.76 (as of 01/31/12)
Ratings:
    The Street: BUY
    Standard & Poor's: STRONG BUY ★ ★ ★ ★ ★
    Ford Equity Research: HOLD
Sector: Industrials
Industry: Construction and Engineering Services
52-Week Range: $30.74 (10/04/11)-Low
                  $52.49 (04/06/11)-High
Shares Outstanding: 128.49M
Beta: 1.29
P/E (Trailing 12-Month): $16.11
EPS (Trailing 12-Month): $2.78
Annual Dividend per Share and Yield: N/A
Market Capitalization: $5.75B
Founded: 1947
Employees: 45,700
Website: http://www.jacobs.com
Address: (U.S.)
Jacobs Engineering Group, Inc.
1111 South Arroyo Parkway
Pasadena, CA 91105
Phone: (626) 578-3500
Investor Relations:
Phone: (626) 578-3500
Company Summary: Jacobs Engineering Group, Inc. provides technical, professional, and construction services to industry and the federal government.

Revenue (Millions $)

Year	1st Q	2nd Q	3rd Q	4th Q	Year Total
2008:	2,471	2,664	2,918	3,196	11,252
2009:	3,232	2,975	2,706	2,552	11,467
2010:	2,477	2,586	2,507	2,343	9,915
2011:	2,356	2,558	2,744	2,723	10,381
2012:	2,631	—	—	—	—

Dividends (none – last paid in 1984)

JOY GLOBAL, INC.

Symbol: JOY (NYSE)
Price: $90.69 (as of 01/31/12)
Ratings:
    The Street: BUY
    Standard & Poor's: BUY ★ ★ ★ ★
    Ford Equity Research: HOLD
Sector: Industrials
Industry: Construction and Farm Machinery
52-Week Range: $57.48 (10/04/11)-Low
                      $103.44 (04/01/11)-High
Shares Outstanding: 105.82M
Beta: 2.09
P/E (Trailing 12-Month): $15.85
EPS (Trailing 12-Month): $5.72
Annual Dividend per Share and Yield: $.70/.80%
Market Capitalization: $9.53B
Founded: 1884
Employees: 14,500
Website: http://www.joyglobal.com
Address: (U.S.)
Joy Global, Inc.
100 East Wisconsin Avenue
Suite 2780
Milwaukee, WI 53202
Phone: (414) 319-8500
Investor Relations:
Phone: (414) 319-8507
E-mail: investor_relations@joyglobal.com
Company Summary: Joy Global, Inc. manufactures and services heavy machinery used in underground and surface mining.

Revenue (Millions $)

Year	1st Q	2nd Q	3rd Q	4th Q	Year Total
2008:	640.3	843.1	903.8	1,031	3,418
2009:	754.9	923.5	956.4	963.5	3,598
2010:	729.2	896.2	850.0	1,049	3,524
2011:	869.5	1,062	1,136	1,335	4,403
2012:	1,136	—	—	—	—

Dividends (per share-last four)

$	Date Declared	Ex-Dividend Date	Date of Record	Payment Date
.175	05/19/11	06/02/11	06/06/11	06/20/11
.175	08/22/11	08/31/11	09/05/11	09/19/11
.175	11/22/11	12/01/11	12/05/11	12/19/11
.175	02/17/12	03/01/12	03/05/12	03/19/12

KLA-TENCOR CORP.
Symbol: KLAC (NASDAQ)
Price: $51.11 (as of 01/31/12)
Ratings:
  The Street: BUY
  Standard & Poor's: BUY ★ ★ ★ ★
  Ford Equity Research: STRONG BUY
Sector: Information Technology
Industry: Semiconductor Equipment and Materials
52-Week Range: $33.20 (09/06/11)-Low
              $53.05 (01/27/12)-High
Shares Outstanding: 166.73M
Beta: 1.78
P/E (Trailing 12-Month): $11.51
EPS (Trailing 12-Month): $4.44
Annual Dividend per Share and Yield: $1.40/2.70%
Market Capitalization: $8.52B
Founded: 1975 (as KLA Instruments)
Employees: 5,500
Website: http://www.kla-tencor.com
Address: (U.S.)
KLA-Tencor Corp.
One Technology Drive
Milpitas, CA 95035
Phone: (408) 875-3000
Investor Relations:
Phone: (408) 875-3000
Company Summary: KLA-Tencor Corp. is a supplier of process control and yield management solutions for the semiconductor and related microelectronics industries.

Revenue (Millions $)

Year	1st Q	2nd Q	3rd Q	4th Q	Year Total
2008:	693.0	635.8	602.2	590.7	2,522
2009:	532.5	396.6	309.6	281.5	1,520
2010:	342.7	440.4	478.3	559.4	1,821
2011:	682.3	766.3	834.1	892.4	3,175
2012:	796.5	642.5	—	—	—

Dividends (per share-last four)

$	Date Declared	Ex-Dividend Date	Date of Record	Payment Date
.25	05/05/11	05/12/11	05/16/11	06/01/11
.35	08/04/11	08/11/11	08/15/11	09/01/11
.35	11/03/11	11/09/11	11/14/11	12/01/11
.35	02/09/12	02/16/12	02/21/12	03/01/12

KOHL'S CORP.

Symbol: KSS (NYSE)
Price: $45.99 (as of 01/31/12)
Ratings:
> **The Street:** BUY
> **Standard & Poor's:** BUY ★ ★ ★ ★ ☆
> **Ford Equity Research:** BUY

Sector: Consumer Services
Industry: Department Stores
52-Week Range: $42.14 (09/12/11)-Low
> $57.39 (07/21/11)-High

Shares Outstanding: 251.00M
Beta: .63
P/E (Trailing 12-Month): $10.81
EPS (Trailing 12-Month): $4.26
Annual Dividend per Share and Yield: $1.00/2.10%
Market Capitalization: $11.66B
Founded: 1962
Employees: 136,000
Website: http://www.kohls.com
Address: (U.S.)
Kohl's Corp.
N56 W17000 Ridgewood Drive
Menomonee Falls, WI 53051
Phone: (262) 703-7000
Investor Relations:
Phone: (262) 703-1440
E-mail: investor.relations@kohls.com
Company Summary: Kohl's Corp. is a department store chain which operates approximately 1,089 stores in 49 states.

Revenue (Millions $)

Year	1st Q	2nd Q	3rd Q	4th Q	Year Total
2008:	3,572	3,589	3,825	5,487	16,473
2009:	3,624	3,725	3,804	5,235	16,389
2010:	3,638	3,807	4,051	5,682	17,178
2011:	4,035	4,100	4,218	6,038	18,391
2012:	4,162	4,248	4,376	6,018	18,804

Dividends (per share-last four)

$	Date Declared	Ex-Dividend Date	Date of Record	Payment Date
.25	05/12/11	06/06/11	06/08/11	06/29/11
.25	08/11/11	09/02/11	09/07/11	09/28/11
.25	11/10/11	12/05/11	12/07/11	12/28/11
.32	02/23/12	03/05/12	03/07/12	03/28/12

LABORATORY CORPORATION OF AMERICA HOLDINGS

Symbol: LH (NYSE)
Price: $91.39 (as of 01/31/12)
Ratings:
   The Street: BUY
   Standard & Poor's: BUY ★ ★ ★ ★ ☆
   Ford Equity Research: STRONG BUY
Sector: Health Care
Industry: Clinical Laboratories and Research
52-Week Range: $74.57 (10/04/11)-Low
                   $100.94 (05/17/11)-High
Shares Outstanding: 97.20M
Beta: .59
P/E (Trailing 12-Month): $18.28
EPS (Trailing 12-Month): $5.00
Annual Dividend per Share and Yield: N/A
Market Capitalization: $9.06B
Founded: 1995 (merger of National Health Laboratories, Inc. and Roche Biomedical Laboratories, Inc.)
Employees: 31,000
Website: http://www.labcorp.com
Address: (U.S.)
Laboratory Corp. of America Holdings
358 South Main Street
Burlington, NC 27215
Phone: (336) 229-1127
Investor Relations:
Phone: (336) 436-5274
E-mail: investor@labcorp.com
Company Summary: Laboratory Corp. of America Holdings operates one of the largest clinical laboratory networks in the world, with a United States network of 36 primary laboratories.

Revenue (Millions $)

Year	1st Q	2nd Q	3rd Q	4th Q	Year Total
2008:	1,103	1,148	1,135	1,119	4,505
2009:	1,156	1,189	1,185	1,165	4,695
2010:	1,194	1,238	1,277	1,295	5,004
2011:	1,368	1,403	1,405	1,366	5,542

Dividends (none)

LIFE TECHNOLOGIES CORP.

Symbol: LIFE (NASDAQ)
Price: $48.43 (as of 01/31/12)
Ratings:
    The Street: BUY
    Standard & Poor's: BUY ★ ★ ★ ★
    Ford Equity Research: HOLD
Sector: Health Care
Industry: Clinical Laboratories and Research
52-Week Range: $35.30 (08/22/11)-Low
                $56.71 (05/13/11)-High
Shares Outstanding: 178.27M
Beta: .52
P/E (Trailing 12-Month): $25.42
EPS (Trailing 12-Month): $1.91
Annual Dividend per Share and Yield: N/A
Market Capitalization: $8.63B
Founded: 1983 (merger of Bethesda Research Laboratories, Inc. and Grand Island Biological Company Corp.)
Employees: 10,400
Website: http://www.lifetechnologies.com
Address: (U.S.)
Life Technologies Corp.
3175 Staley Road
Grand Island, NY 14072
Phone: (800) 955-6288
Investor Relations:
Phone: (800) 955-6288
Company Summary: Life Technologies Corp. is a biotechnology company that develops and manufactures research products and instruments.

Revenue (Millions $)

Year	1st Q	2nd Q	3rd Q	4th Q	Year Total
2008:	350.2	367.8	361.4	540.6	1,620
2009:	775.7	832.8	800.7	871.1	3,280
2010:	884.9	903.7	867.1	932.3	3,588
2011:	895.9	941.1	928.2	1,010	3,775

Dividends (none)

LORILLARD, INC.

Symbol: LO (NYSE)
Price: $107.39 (as of 01/31/12)
Ratings:
>**The Street:** BUY
>**Standard & Poor's:** BUY ★ ★ ★ ★
>**Ford Equity Research:** STRONG BUY

Sector: Consumer Goods
Industry: Tobacco
52-Week Range: $93.32 (03/24/11)-Low
$115.67 (01/10/12)-High
Shares Outstanding: 130.89M
Beta: .29
P/E (Trailing 12-Month): $14.46
EPS (Trailing 12-Month): $7.43
Annual Dividend per Share and Yield: $5.20/4.80%
Market Capitalization: $14.50B
Founded: 1760
Employees: 2,800
Website: http://www.lorillard.com
Address: (U.S.)
Lorillard, Inc.
714 Green Valley Road
Greensboro, NC 27408-7018
Phone: (336) 335-7000
Investor Relations:
Phone: (336) 335-7665
E-mail: investorrelations@lortobco.com
Company Summary: Lorillard, Inc. is a tobacco company
marketing cigarettes under the brand names Newport,
Maverick, Old Gold, Kent, True, Satin, and Max.

Revenue (Millions $)

Year	1st Q	2nd Q	3rd Q	4th Q	Year Total
2008:	921	1,070	1,125	1,088	4,204
2009:	917	1,519	1,419	1,378	5,233
2010:	1,360	1,519	1,567	1,486	5,932
2011:	1,535	1,692	1,622	1,617	6,466

Dividends (per share-last four)

$	Date Declared	Ex-Dividend Date	Date of Record	Payment Date
1.30	02/17/11	02/25/11	03/01/11	03/11/11
1.30	05/19/11	05/27/11	06/01/11	06/10/11
1.30	11/09/11	11/29/11	12/01/11	12/12/11
1.55	02/08/12	02/28/12	03/01/12	03/09/12

MASCO CORP.

Symbol: MAS (NYSE)
Price: $12.07 (as of 01/31/12)
Ratings:
   The Street: HOLD
   Standard & Poor's: BUY ★ ★ ★ ★
   Ford Equity Research: HOLD
Sector: Industrials
Industry: Building Materials
52-Week Range: $6.60 (10/04/11)-Low
                $14.43 (05/31/11)-High
Shares Outstanding: 357.29M
Beta: 2.63
P/E (Trailing 12-Month): N/A
EPS (Trailing 12-Month): $-2.99
Annual Dividend per Share and Yield: $.30/2.40%
Market Capitalization: $4.32B
Founded: 1929
Employees: 31,000
Website: http://www.masco.com
Address: (U.S.)
Masco Corp.
21001 Van Born Road
Taylor, MI 48180
Phone: (313) 274-7400
Investor Relations:
Phone: (313) 792-5500
E-mail: maria_duey@mascohq.com
Company Summary: Masco Corp. focuses on manufacturing and distribution of building products and branded consumer products for the home improvement and construction markets.

Revenue (Millions $)

Year	1st Q	2nd Q	3rd Q	4th Q	Year Total
2008:	2,446	2,640	2,535	1,979	9,600
2009:	1,797	2,013	2,084	1,763	7,657
2010:	1,852	2,048	1,957	1,629	7,486
2011:	1,772	2,022	2,006	1,667	7,467

Dividends (per share-last four)

$	Date Declared	Ex-Dividend Date	Date of Record	Payment Date
.075	03/25/11	04/06/11	04/08/11	05/09/11
.075	06/24/11	07/06/11	07/08/11	08/08/11
.075	09/09/11	10/05/11	10/07/11	11/07/11
.075	12/06/11	01/04/12	01/06/12	02/06/12

MCCORMICK & CO., INC.

Symbol: MKC (NYSE)
Price: $50.54 (as of 01/31/12)
Ratings:
  The Street: BUY
  Standard & Poor's: HOLD ★ ★ ★
  Ford Equity Research: HOLD
Sector: Consumer Goods
Industry: Processed and Packaged Foods
52-Week Range: $43.36 (08/09/11)-Low
                   $52.21 (01/19/12)-High
Shares Outstanding: 133.05M
Beta: .24
P/E (Trailing 12-Month): $18.11
EPS (Trailing 12-Month): $2.79
Annual Dividend per Share and Yield: $1.24/2.50%
Market Capitalization: $6.72B
Founded: 1889
Employees: 9,000
Website: http://www.mccormickcorporation.com
Address: (U.S.)
McCormick & Co., Inc.
18 Loveton Circle
Sparks, MD 21152
Phone: (410) 771-7301
Investor Relations:
Phone: (410) 771-7301
Company Summary: McCormick & Co., Inc. manufactures spices, herbs, and flavorings for retail, commercial, and industrial markets.

Revenue (Millions $)

Year	1st Q	2nd Q	3rd Q	4th Q	Year Total
2008:	724.0	964.1	781.6	906.9	3,377
2009:	718.5	757.3	791.7	924.5	3,192
2010:	764.5	798.3	794.6	979.4	3,337
2011:	782.8	883.7	920.4	1,110	3,697

Dividends (per share-last four)

$	Date Declared	Ex-Dividend Date	Date of Record	Payment Date
.28	03/30/11	04/07/11	04/11/11	04/25/11
.28	06/28/11	07/07/11	07/11/11	07/25/11
.28	09/27/11	10/05/11	10/10/11	10/24/11
.31	11/22/11	12/28/11	12/30/11	01/13/12

MCDONALD'S CORP.

Symbol: MCD (NYSE)
Price: $ (as of 01/31/12)
Ratings:
  The Street: BUY
  Standard & Poor's: STRONG BUY ★ ★ ★ ★ ★
  Ford Equity Research: BUY
Sector: Consumer Services
Industry: Restaurants
52-Week Range: $75.46 (03/30/11)-Low
              $102.22 (01/20/12)-High
Shares Outstanding: 1.02B
Beta: .36
P/E (Trailing 12-Month): $18.80
EPS (Trailing 12-Month): $5.27
Annual Dividend per Share and Yield: $2.80/2.80%
Market Capitalization: $101.35B
Founded: 1940
Employees: 420,000
Website: http://www.aboutmcdonalds.com
Address: (U.S.)
McDonald's Corp.
One McDonald
Oak Brook, IL 60523
Phone: (630) 623-3000
Investor Relations:
Phone: (630) 623-3000
Company Summary: McDonald's Corp. is the world's largest fast food company, with more than 33,000 restaurants serving nearly 68 million people in 119 countries each day.

Revenue (Millions $)

Year	1st Q	2nd Q	3rd Q	4th Q	Year Total
2008:	5,615	6,075	6,267	5,565	23,522
2009:	5,077	5,647	6,047	5,973	22,744
2010:	5,610	5,945	6,305	6,214	24,074
2011:	6,112	6,905	7,166	6,822	27,006

Dividends (per share-last four)

$	Date Declared	Ex-Dividend Date	Date of Record	Payment Date
.61	05/18/11	05/27/11	06/01/11	06/15/11
.61	07/21/11	08/30/11	09/01/11	09/16/11
.70	09/22/11	11/29/11	12/01/11	12/15/11
.70	01/26/12	02/28/12	03/01/12	03/15/12

MCKESSON CORP.

Symbol: MCK (NYSE)
Price: $81.72 (as of 01/31/12)
Ratings:
  The Street: BUY
  Standard & Poor's: STRONG BUY ★ ★ ★ ★ ★
  Ford Equity Research: STRONG BUY
Sector: Health Care
Industry: Health Care Distributors
52-Week Range: $66.61 (10/06/11)-Low
  $83.29 (01/31/12)-High
Shares Outstanding: 246.10M
Beta: .48
P/E (Trailing 12-Month): $18.04
EPS (Trailing 12-Month): $4.53
Annual Dividend per Share and Yield: $.80/1.00%
Market Capitalization: $20.07B
Founded: 1833 (as Olcott & McKesson)
Employees: 36,400
Website: http://www.mckesson.com
Address: (U.S.)
McKesson Corp.
McKesson Plaza
One Post Street
San Francisco, CA 94104
Phone: (415) 983-8300
Investor Relations:
Phone: (800) 826-9360
E-mail investors@mckesson.com
Company Summary: McKesson Corp. is a pharmaceuticals company which provides medicines, pharmaceutical supplies, and information and care management services in the health care industry.

Revenue (Millions $)

Year	1st Q	2nd Q	3rd Q	4th Q	Year Total
2008:	24,528	24,450	26,494	26,231	101,703
2009:	26,704	26,574	27,130	26,224	106,632
2010:	26,657	27,130	28,272	26,643	108,702
2011:	27,450	27,534	28,247	28,853	112,084
2012:	29,980	30,216	30,839	—	—

Dividends (per share-last four)

$	Date Declared	Ex-Dividend Date	Date of Record	Payment Date
.20	05/26/11	06/08/11	06/10/11	07/01/11
.20	07/27/11	08/30/11	09/01/11	10/03/11
.20	10/28/11	11/29/11	12/01/11	01/03/12
.20	01/25/12	02/28/12	03/01/12	04/02/12

MERCK & CO., INC.

Symbol: MRK (NYSE)
Price: $38.27 (as of 01/31/12)
Ratings:
    The Street: BUY
    Standard & Poor's: BUY ★ ★ ★ ★
    Ford Equity Research: BUY
Sector: Health Care
Industry: Pharmaceuticals
52-Week Range: $29.47 (08/09/11)-Low
                   $39.43 (01/19/12)-High
Shares Outstanding: 3.04B
Beta: .54
P/E (Trailing 12-Month): $27.98
EPS (Trailing 12-Month): $1.37
Annual Dividend per Share and Yield: $1.68/4.40%
Market Capitalization: $116.64B
Founded: 1891 (as a subsidiary of Merck KGaA)
Employees: 86,000
Website: http://www.merck.com
Address: (U.S.)
Merck & Co., Inc.
One Merck Drive
PO Box 100
Whitehouse Station, NJ 08889-0100
Phone: (908) 423-1000
Investor Relations:
Phone: (800) 522-9114
Company Summary: Merck & Co., Inc., dba Merck Sharp & Dohme, MSD outside the United States and Canada, is one of the largest pharmaceutical companies in the world. The company discovers, develops, manufactures and markets a broad range of innovative products to improve human and animal health. Merck also publishes The Merck Manuals, a series of medical reference books for physicians, nurses, and technicians. These include the *Merck Manual of Diagnosis and Therapy* and the *Merck Index*.

Revenue (Millions $)

Year	1st Q	2nd Q	3rd Q	4th Q	Year Total
2008:	4,657	4,920	4,577	4,348	18,502
2009:	5,385	5,899	6,050	10,094	27,428
2010:	11,422	11,346	11,124	12,094	45,986
2011:	11,580	12,151	12,022	12,294	48,047

Dividends (per share-last four)

$	Date Declared	Ex-Dividend Date	Date of Record	Payment Date
.38	02/22/11	03/11/11	03/15/11	04/07/11
.38	07/26/11	09/13/11	09/15/11	10/07/11
.42	11/10/11	12/13/11	12/15/11	01/09/12
.42	02/28/12	03/13/12	03/15/12	04/06/12

METLIFE, INC.

Symbol: MET (NYSE)
Price: $35.33 (as of 01/31/12)
Ratings:

   The Street: BUY
   Standard & Poor's: BUY ★ ★ ★ ★
   Ford Equity Research: STRONG BUY
Sector: Financials
Industry: Life Insurance and Financial Services
52-Week Range: $25.61 (10/04/11)-Low
                  $47.10 (05/02/11)-High
Shares Outstanding: 1.06B
Beta: 2.18
P/E (Trailing 12-Month): $6.61
EPS (Trailing 12-Month): $5.34
Annual Dividend per Share and Yield: $.74/2.10%
Market Capitalization: $37.37B
Founded: 1868
Employees: 66,000
Website: http://www.metlife.com
Address: (U.S.)
MetLife, Inc.
200 Park Avenue
New York, NY 10166-0188
Phone: (212) 578-2211
Investor Relations:
Phone: (212) 578-2211
Company Summary: MetLife, Inc. is a provider of insurance, annuities, and employee benefit programs.

Revenue (Millions $)

Year	1st Q	2nd Q	3rd Q	4th Q	Year Total
2008:	13,027	13,714	10,363	13,885	50,989
2009:	10,214	8,265	10,238	11,940	40,657
2010:	13,100	14,137	12,338	12,690	52,265
2011:	15,912	17,149	20,456	16,745	70,262

Dividends (per share-last four)

$	Date Declared	Ex-Dividend Date	Date of Record	Payment Date
.74	10/28/08	11/06/08	11/10/08	12/15/08
.74	10/29/09	11/05/09	11/09/09	12/14/09
.74	10/26/10	11/05/10	11/09/10	12/14/10
.74	10/25/11	11/07/11	11/09/11	12/14/11

MICROSOFT CORP.

Symbol: MSFT (NASDAQ)
Price: $29.53 (as of 01/31/12)
Ratings:
  The Street: BUY
  Standard & Poor's: BUY ★ ★ ★ ★ ☆
  Ford Equity Research: HOLD
Sector: Information Technology
Industry: Application Software
52-Week Range: $23.65 (06/16/11)-Low
              $29.95 (01/23/12)-High
Shares Outstanding: 8.39B
Beta: .98
P/E (Trailing 12-Month): $10.70
EPS (Trailing 12-Month): $2.76
Annual Dividend per Share and Yield: $.80/2.70%
Market Capitalization: $247.78B
Founded: 1975
Employees: 90,000
Website: http://www.microsoft.com
Address: (U.S.)
Microsoft Corp.
One Microsoft Way
Redmond, WA 98052-6399
Phone: (425) 882-8080
Investor Relations:
Phone: (800) 285-7772
E-mail: msft@microsoft.com
Company Summary: Microsoft Corp. develops, manufactures, licenses, and supports a wide range of products and services predominantly related to computing through its various product divisions. The company is well known for its PC software, namely the Windows operating system.

Revenue (Millions $)

Year	1st Q	2nd Q	3rd Q	4th Q	Year Total
2008:	13,762	16,367	14,454	15,837	60,420
2009:	15,061	16,629	13,648	13,099	58,437
2010:	12,920	19,022	14,503	16,039	62,484
2011:	16,195	19,953	16,428	17,367	69,943
2012:	17,372	20,885	—	—	—

Dividends (per share-last four)

$	Date Declared	Ex-Dividend Date	Date of Record	Payment Date
.16	06/15/11	08/16/11	08/18/11	09/08/11
.20	09/20/11	11/15/11	11/17/11	12/08/11
.20	12/14/11	02/14/12	02/16/12	03/08/12
.20	03/13/12	05/15/12	05/17/12	06/14/12

MOSAIC CO.

Symbol: MOS (NYSE)
Price: $55.97 (as of 01/31/12)
Ratings:
> **The Street:** BUY
> **Standard & Poor's:** BUY ★ ★ ★ ★
> **Ford Equity Research:** HOLD

Sector: Materials
Industry: Agricultural Chemicals
52-Week Range: $44.86 (10/04/11)-Low
$83.41 (04/05/11)-High
Shares Outstanding: 425.41M
Beta: .88
P/E (Trailing 12-Month): $10.68
EPS (Trailing 12-Month): $5.24
Annual Dividend per Share and Yield: $.20/.40%
Market Capitalization: $23.81B
Founded: 2004
Employees: 7,700
Website: http://www.mosaicco.com
Address: (U.S.)
The Mosaic Co.
3033 Campus Drive
Atria Corporate Center
Plymouth, MN 55441
Phone: (763) 577-2700
Investor Relations:
Phone: (763) 577-8213
E-mail: investor@mosaicco.com
Company Summary: The Mosaic Co. produces and markets two crop nutrients, phosphate and potash. The company also produces K-Mag, MicroEssentials and Pegasus.

Revenue (Millions $)

Year	1st Q	2nd Q	3rd Q	4th Q	Year Total
2008:	2,003	2,195	2,147	3,467	9,812
2009:	4,322	3,006	1,376	1,594	10,298
2010:	1,457	1,710	1,732	1,860	6,759
2011:	2,188	2,675	2,214	2,860	9,937
2012:	3,083	3,014	—	—	—

Dividends (per share-last three)

$	Date Declared	Ex-Dividend Date	Date of Record	Payment Date
.05	07/21/11	08/02/11	08/04/11	08/18/11
.05	10/12/11	11/01/11	11/03/11	11/17/11
.05	12/08/11	01/31/12	02/02/12	02/16/12

NATIONAL OILWELL VARCO, INC.

Symbol: NOV (NYSE)
Price: $73.98 (as of 01/31/12)
Ratings:
    The Street: BUY
    Standard & Poor's: BUY ★ ★ ★ ★
    Ford Equity Research: BUY
Sector: Energy
Industry: Oil and Gas Equipment and Services
52-Week Range: $47.97 (10/04/11)-Low
                 $78.45 (01/26/12)-High
Shares Outstanding: 423.13M
Beta: 1.49
P/E (Trailing 12-Month): $16.81
EPS (Trailing 12-Month): $4.40
Annual Dividend per Share and Yield: $.48/.60%
Market Capitalization: $31.36B
Founded: 1908 (as the Abegg and Reinhold Company)
Employees: 42,183
Website: http://www.nov.com
Address: (U.S.)
National Oilwell Varco, Inc.
7909 Parkwood Circle Drive
Houston, TX 77036-6565
Phone: (713) 346-7500
Investor Relations:
Phone: (713) 346-7500
E-mail: investor.relations@natoil.com
Company Summary: National Oilwell Varco, Inc. manufactures land-based and offshore oil drilling rigs as well as all the major mechanical components for oil rigs. The company also performs well and pipeline inspections, manufactures and sales equipment and components used in oil and gas drilling and production, and offers supply chain integration services to the oil and gas industry.

National Oilwell Varco, Inc. (NOV)

Revenue (Millions $)

Year	1st Q	2nd Q	3rd Q	4th Q	Year Total
2008:	2,685	3,324	3,612	3,810	13,431
2009:	3,481	3,010	3,087	3,134	12,712
2010:	3,032	2,941	3,011	3,172	12,156
2011:	3,146	3,513	3,740	4,259	14,658

Dividends (per share-last four)

$	Date Declared	Ex-Dividend Date	Date of Record	Payment Date
.11	05/12/11	06/08/11	06/10/11	06/24/11
.11	08/18/11	09/07/11	09/09/11	09/23/11
.12	11/17/11	11/30/11	12/02/11	12/16/11
.12	02/23/12	03/14/12	03/16/12	03/30/12

NORDSTROM, INC.

Symbol: JWN (NYSE)
Price: $49.38 (as of 01/31/12)
Ratings:
    The Street: BUY
    Standard & Poor's: HOLD ★ ★ ★ ☆ ☆
    Ford Equity Research: BUY
Sector: Consumer Goods
Industry: Department Stores
52-Week Range: $37.28 (08/19/11)-Low
                     $53.35 (10/24/11)-High
Shares Outstanding: 207.92M
Beta: 1.36
P/E (Trailing 12-Month): $16.01
EPS (Trailing 12-Month): $3.08
Annual Dividend per Share and Yield: $.92/1.90%
Market Capitalization: $10.34B
Founded: 1901
Employees: 61,500
Website: http://www.nordstrom.com
Address: (U.S.)
Nordstrom, Inc.
1617 Sixth Avenue
Suite 500
Seattle, WA 98101
Phone: (206) 628-2111
Investor Relations:
Phone: (206) 233-6564
E-mail: invrelations@nordstrom.com
Company Summary: Nordstrom, Inc. is a department store chain that sells clothing, accessories, handbags, jewelry, cosmetics, fragrances, and home furnishings.

Revenue (Millions $)

Year	1st Q	2nd Q	3rd Q	4th Q	Year Total
2008:	1,954	2,390	1,970	2,514	8,828
2009:	1,949	2,359	1,879	2,386	8,573
2010:	1,792	2,232	1,963	2,640	8,627
2011:	2,087	2,515	2,182	2,916	9,700
2012:	2,323	2,810	2,478	3,266	10,877

Dividends (per share-last four)

$	Date Declared	Ex-Dividend Date	Date of Record	Payment Date
.23	05/11/11	05/26/11	05/31/11	06/15/11
.23	08/24/11	09/01/11	09/06/11	09/15/11
.23	11/18/11	11/28/11	11/30/11	12/15/11
.27	02/17/12	02/28/12	03/01/12	03/15/12

NORFOLK SOUTHERN CORP.

Symbol: NSC (NYSE)
Price: $72.20 (as of 01/31/12)
Ratings:
   The Street: BUY
   Standard & Poor's: BUY ★ ★ ★ ★
   Ford Equity Research: BUY
Sector: Industrials
Industry: Railroads
52-Week Range: $57.57 (10/04/11)-Low
                  $78.50 (01/12/12)-High
Shares Outstanding: 330.14M
Beta: 1.29
P/E (Trailing 12-Month): $13.25
EPS (Trailing 12-Month): $5.45
Annual Dividend per Share and Yield: $1.88/2.50%
Market Capitalization: $23.85B
Founded: 1982
Employees: 30,329
Website: http://www.nscorp.com
Address: (U.S.)
Norfolk Southern Corp.
Three Commercial Place
Norfolk, VA 23510-2191
Phone: (757) 629-2680
Investor Relations:
Phone: (757) 629-2861
Company Summary: Norfolk Southern Corp. is a railroad that operates along a 20,000 mile route encompassing 22 eastern states and Ontario, Canada.

Revenue (Millions $)

Year	1st Q	2nd Q	3rd Q	4th Q	Year Total
2008:	2,500	2,765	2,894	2,502	10,661
2009:	1,943	1,857	2,063	2,106	7,969
2010:	2,238	2,430	2,456	2,392	9,516
2011:	2,620	2,866	2,889	2,797	11,172

Dividends (per share-last four)

$	Date Declared	Ex-Dividend Date	Date of Record	Payment Date
.40	04/26/11	05/04/11	05/06/11	06/10/11
.43	07/26/11	08/03/11	08/05/11	09/10/11
.43	10/25/11	11/02/11	11/04/11	12/10/11
.47	01/24/12	02/01/12	02/03/12	03/10/12

OMNICOM GROUP, INC.

Symbol: OMC (NYSE)
Price: $45.61 (as of 01/31/12)
Ratings:
    The Street: BUY
    Standard & Poor's: BUY ★ ★ ★ ★
    Ford Equity Research: HOLD
Sector: Consumer Services
Industry: Advertising
52-Week Range: $35.27 (09/22/11)-Low
                  $51.25 (03/01/11)-High
Shares Outstanding: 272.80M
Beta: 1.31
P/E (Trailing 12-Month): $14.26
EPS (Trailing 12-Month): $3.20
Annual Dividend per Share and Yield: $1.00/2.10%
Market Capitalization: $12.58B
Founded: 1986
Employees: 70,600
Website: http://www.omnicomgroup.com
Address: (U.S.)
Omnicom Group, Inc.
437 Madison Avenue
New York, NY 10022
Phone: (212) 415-3600
Investor Relations:
E-mail: IR@OmnicomGroup.com
Company Summary: Omnicom Group, Inc. is a holding company whose agencies provide marketing and communications services in the areas of advertising, customer relationship management (CRM), strategic media planning and buying, digital and interactive marketing, direct and promotional marketing and public relations.

Revenue (Millions $)

Year	1st Q	2nd Q	3rd Q	4th Q	Year Total
2008:	3,195	3,476	3,316	3,371	13,359
2009:	2,746	2,870	2,838	3,266	11,720
2010:	2,920	3,041	2,994	3,587	12,542
2011:	3,151	3,487	3,380	3,852	13,872

Dividends (per share-last four)

$	Date Declared	Ex-Dividend Date	Date of Record	Payment Date
.25	05/25/11	06/10/11	06/14/11	07/11/11
.25	07/21/11	09/21/11	09/23/11	10/07/11
.25	12/08/11	12/19/11	12/21/11	01/09/12
.30	02/08/12	03/01/12	03/05/12	04/02/12

ONEOK, INC.

Symbol: OKE (NYSE)
Price: $83.16 (as of 01/31/12)
Ratings:

> **The Street:** BUY
> **Standard & Poor's:** HOLD ★ ★ ★
> **Ford Equity Research:** BUY

Sector: Utilities
Industry: Gas Utilities
52-Week Range: $58.61 (08/09/11)-Low
$89.63 (01/17/12)-High
Shares Outstanding: 103.89M
Beta: 1.16
P/E (Trailing 12-Month): $27.36
EPS (Trailing 12-Month): $3.04
Annual Dividend per Share and Yield: $2.44/2.90%
Market Capitalization: $8.56B
Founded: 1906
Employees: 4,795
Website: http://www.oneok.com
Address: (U.S.)
ONEOK, Inc.
100 West Fifth Street
Tulsa, OK 74103
Phone: (918) 588-7000
Investor Relations:
Phone: (918) 588-7950
E-mail: DHarrison@oneok.com
Company Summary: ONEOK, Inc. is a diversified natural gas distributor and serves approximately 2 million customers through its natural gas distribution companies Oklahoma Natural Gas, Kansas Gas Service, and Texas Gas Service.

Revenue (Millions $)

Year	1st Q	2nd Q	3rd Q	4th Q	Year Total
2008:	4,902	4,173	4,239	2,843	16,157
2009:	2,790	2,228	2,364	3,423	10,805
2010:	3,924	2,807	2,943	3,004	12,678
2011:	3,867	3,514	3,595	3,829	14,805

Dividends (per share-last four)

$	Date Declared	Ex-Dividend Date	Date of Record	Payment Date
.52	04/19/11	04/27/11	04/29/11	05/13/11
.56	07/20/11	07/28/11	08/01/11	08/12/11
.56	10/26/11	11/03/11	11/07/11	11/14/11
.61	01/18/12	01/27/12	01/31/12	02/14/12

ORACLE CORP.

Symbol: ORCL (NASDAQ)
Price: $28.60 (as of 01/31/12)
Ratings:
   The Street: BUY
   Standard & Poor's: BUY ★ ★ ★ ★
   Ford Equity Research: HOLD
Sector: Information Technology
Industry: Application Software
52-Week Range: $24.72 (08/18/11)-Low
                         $36.50 (05/03/11)-High
Shares Outstanding: 4.98B
Beta: 1.15
P/E (Trailing 12-Month): $15.52
EPS (Trailing 12-Month): $1.82
Annual Dividend per Share and Yield: $.24/.80%
Market Capitalization: $141.78B
Founded: 1977
Employees: 108,000
Website: http://www.oracle.com
Address: (U.S.)
Oracle Corp.
500 Oracle Parkway
Redwood City, CA 94065
Phone: (650) 506-7000
Investor Relations:
Phone: (650) 506-4073
Email: investor_us@oracle.com
Company Summary: Oracle Corp. is a computer
technology company that specializes in developing and
marketing computer hardware systems and software
products, specifically database management systems.

Revenue (Millions $)

Year	1st Q	2nd Q	3rd Q	4th Q	Year Total
2008:	4,529	5,313	5,349	7,239	22,430
2009:	5,331	5,607	5,453	6,861	23,252
2010:	5,054	5,857	6,404	9,505	26,820
2011:	7,502	8,582	8,763	10,775	35,622
2012:	8,374	8,792	9,039	—	—

Dividends (per share-last four)

$	Date Declared	Ex-Dividend Date	Date of Record	Payment Date
.06	03/22/11	04/11/11	04/13/11	05/04/11
.06	06/22/11	07/11/11	07/13/11	08/03/11
.06	09/20/11	10/07/11	10/12/11	11/02/11
.06	12/19/11	01/09/12	01/11/12	02/01/12

PACCAR, INC.

Symbol: PCAR (NASDAQ)
Price: $44.20 (as of 01/31/12)
Ratings:
  The Street: BUY
  Standard & Poor's: STRONG BUY ★ ★ ★ ★ ★
  Ford Equity Research: HOLD
Sector: Industrials
Industry: Farm Machinery and Heavy Trucks
52-Week Range: $31.57 (10/04/11)-Low
$54.58 (04/28/11)-High
Shares Outstanding: 356.88M
Beta: 1.42
P/E (Trailing 12-Month): $18.35
EPS (Trailing 12-Month): $2.41
Annual Dividend per Share and Yield: $.72/1.60%
Market Capitalization: $15.83B
Founded: 1905
Employees: 23,400
Website: http://www.paccar.com
Address: (U.S.)
PACCAR, Inc.
777-106th Avenue NE
Bellevue, WA 98004
Phone: (425) 468-7400
Investor Relations:
Phone: (425) 468-7400
Company Summary: PACCAR, Inc. is a manufacturer of heavy-duty trucks which includes the Peterbilt and Kenworth brands.

Revenue (Millions $)

Year	1st Q	2nd Q	3rd Q	4th Q	Year Total
2008:	3,938	4,112	4,005	2,917	14,972
2009:	1,854	1,721	1,888	1,612	7,076
2010:	2,120	2,359	2,440	2,404	9,325
2011:	3,182	3,855	4,150	4,137	15,325

Dividends (per share-last four)

$	Date Declared	Ex-Dividend Date	Date of Record	Payment Date
.18	07/11/11	08/16/11	08/18/11	09/06/11
.18	09/13/11	11/16/11	11/18/11	12/05/11
.70	12/06/11	12/15/11	12/19/11	01/05/12
.18	12/06/11	02/15/12	02/17/12	03/05/12

PEABODY ENERGY CORP.

Symbol: BTU (NYSE)
Price: $34.09 (as of 01/31/12)
Ratings:
   The Street: HOLD
   Standard & Poor's: HOLD ★ ★ ★
   Ford Equity Research: HOLD
Sector: Energy
Industry: Industrial Minerals
52-Week Range: $30.60 (10/04/11)-Low
                   $73.95 (04/04/11)-High
Shares Outstanding: 272.26M
Beta: 1.4
P/E (Trailing 12-Month): $9.68
EPS (Trailing 12-Month): $3.52
Annual Dividend per Share and Yield: $.34/.90%
Market Capitalization: $9.21B
Founded: 1883
Employees: 8,300
Website: http://www.peabodyenergy.com
Address: (U.S.)
Peabody Energy Corp.
701 Market Street
St Louis, MO 63101-1826
Phone: (314) 342-3400
Investor Relations:
Phone: (314) 342-7900
E-mail: ir@peabodyenergy.com
Company Summary: Peabody Energy Corp. is a private-sector coal company which engages in the mining and sale and distribution of coal. The company also markets, brokers and trades coal through offices in China, Australia, Germany, the United Kingdom, Indonesia, Singapore and the United States.

Revenue (Millions $)

Year	1st Q	2nd Q	3rd Q	4th Q	Year Total
2008:	1,275	1,531	1,906	1,881	6,593
2009:	1,453	1,338	1,667	1,388	5,847
2010:	1,516	1,661	1,864	1,698	6,739
2011:	1,745	2,008	2,036	2,185	7,974

Dividends (per share-last four)

$	Date Declared	Ex-Dividend Date	Date of Record	Payment Date
.085	05/03/11	05/13/11	05/17/11	06/07/11
.085	07/22/11	08/02/11	08/04/11	08/25/11
.085	10/20/11	11/01/11	11/03/11	11/25/11
.085	01/26/12	02/07/12	02/09/12	03/01/12

PEPSICO, INC.
Symbol: PEP (NYSE)
Price: $65.67 (as of 01/31/12)
Ratings:
  The Street: BUY
  Standard & Poor's: BUY ★ ★ ★ ★
  Ford Equity Research: HOLD
Sector: Consumer Goods
Industry: Soft Drinks
52-Week Range: $58.50 (10/04/11)-Low
  $71.89 (05/19/11)-High
Shares Outstanding: 1.57B
Beta: .42
P/E (Trailing 12-Month): $16.46
EPS (Trailing 12-Month): $3.99
Annual Dividend per Share and Yield: $2.06/3.10%
Market Capitalization: $102.67B
Founded: 1965
Employees: 297,000
Website: http://www.pepsico.com
Address: (U.S.)
PepsiCo, Inc.
700 Anderson Hill Road
Purchase, NY 10577
Phone: (914) 253-2000
Investor Relations:
E-mail: investor@pepsico.com
Company Summary: PepsiCo, Inc. engages in the manufacturing, marketing and distribution of beverages and grain-based snack foods.

Revenue (Millions $)

Year	1st Q	2nd Q	3rd Q	4th Q	Year Total
2008:	8,333	10,945	11,244	12,729	43,251
2009:	8,263	10,592	11,080	13,297	43,232
2010:	9,368	14,801	15,514	18,155	57,838
2011:	11,937	16,827	17,582	20,158	66,504

Dividends (per share-last four)

$	Date Declared	Ex-Dividend Date	Date of Record	Payment Date
.515	05/04/11	06/01/11	06/03/11	06/30/11
.515	07/15/11	08/31/11	09/02/11	09/30/11
.515	11/17/11	11/30/11	12/02/11	01/03/12
.515	02/03/12	02/29/12	03/02/12	03/30/12

REYNOLDS AMERICAN, INC.

Symbol: RAI (NYSE)
Price: $39.23 (as of 01/31/12)
Ratings:
> **The Street:** BUY
> **Standard & Poor's:** BUY ★ ★ ★ ★
> **Ford Equity Research:** STRONG BUY

Sector: Consumer Goods
Industry: Tobacco
52-Week Range: $31.82 (08/09/11)-Low
> $41.95 (12/29/11)-High

Shares Outstanding: 576.14M
Beta: .63
P/E (Trailing 12-Month): $17.28
EPS (Trailing 12-Month): $2.27
Annual Dividend per Share and Yield: $2.24/5.70%
Market Capitalization: $22.87B
Founded: 2004 (by merger with British American Tobacco (Brown & Williamson) and R. J. Reynolds Tobacco Company)
Employees: 5,400
Website: http://www.reynoldsamerican.com
Address: (U.S.)
Reynolds American, Inc.
401 North Main Street
Winston-Salem, NC 27101
Phone: (336) 741-2000
Investor Relations:
Phone: (336) 741-5165
E-mail: raiinvestorrelations@reynoldsamerican.com
Company Summary: Reynolds American, Inc. is a tobacco company in the United States with holdings that include R. J. Reynolds Tobacco Company, American Snuff Company, Santa Fe Natural Tobacco Company and Niconovum AB. Reynolds American's subsidiaries manufacture and market a variety of tobacco products, including cigarettes such as the Camel, Pall Mall, Kool, Winston, Salem, Doral, Misty,

Capri and Natural American Spirit brands and moist snuff
(Grizzly and Kodiak brands).

Revenue (Millions $)

Year	1st Q	2nd Q	3rd Q	4th Q	Year Total
2008:	2,057	2,339	2,272	2,177	8,845
2009:	1,921	2,449	2,259	1,912	8,541
2010:	1,986	2,245	2,239	2,081	8,551
2011:	1,991	2,267	2,200	1,961	8,419

Dividends (per share-last four)

$	Date Declared	Ex-Dividend Date	Date of Record	Payment Date
.53	05/06/11	06/08/11	06/10/11	07/01/11
.53	07/15/11	09/08/11	09/12/11	10/03/11
.56	10/25/11	12/07/11	12/09/11	01/03/12
.56	02/02/12	03/07/12	03/09/12	04/02/12

ROBERT HALF INTERNATIONAL, INC.

Symbol: RHI (NYSE)
Price: $27.69 (as of 01/31/12)
Ratings:

The Street: BUY

Standard & Poor's: BUY ★ ★ ★ ★

Ford Equity Research: SELL

Sector: Industrials
Industry: Employment Services
52-Week Range: $19.69 (09/23/11)-Low
$31.83 (04/06/11)-High
Shares Outstanding: 139.17M
Beta: 1.56
P/E (Trailing 12-Month): $26.63
EPS (Trailing 12-Month): $1.04
Annual Dividend per Share and Yield: $.56/2.00%
Market Capitalization: $3.96B
Founded: 1948
Employees: 11,300 (full-time)
Website: http://www.rhi.com
Address: (U.S.)
Robert Half International, Inc.
2884 Sand Hill Road
Suite 200
Menlo Park, CA 94025
Phone: (650) 234-6000
Investor Relations:
Phone: (650) 234-6000
E-mail: investor.relations@rhi.com
Company Summary: Robert Half International, Inc. is an accounting and finance staffing firm providing businesses with temporary and permanent personnel.

Robert Half International, Inc. (RHI)

Revenue (Millions $)

Year	1st Q	2nd Q	3rd Q	4th Q	Year Total
2008:	1,225	1,225	1,160	990	4,600
2009:	823	750	726	737	3,036
2010:	737	769	817	852	3,175
2011:	881	938	985	973	3,776

Dividends (per share-last four)

$	Date Declared	Ex-Dividend Date	Date of Record	Payment Date
.14	05/04/11	05/23/11	05/25/11	06/15/11
.14	07/27/11	08/23/11	08/25/11	09/15/11
.14	11/02/11	11/21/11	11/23/11	12/15/11
.15	02/08/12	02/22/12	02/24/12	03/15/12

ROCKWELL AUTOMATION, INC.

Symbol: ROK (NYSE)
Price: $77.87 (as of 01/31/12)
Ratings:
   The Street: BUY
   Standard & Poor's: STRONG BUY ★ ★ ★ ★ ★
   Ford Equity Research: BUY
Sector: Industrials
Industry: Industrial Electrical Equipment
52-Week Range: $50.36 (09/22/11)-Low
                   $98.19 (04/26/11)-High
Shares Outstanding: 142.39M
Beta: 1.93
P/E (Trailing 12-Month): $15.33
EPS (Trailing 12-Month): $5.08
Annual Dividend per Share and Yield: $1.70/2.20%
Market Capitalization: $11.21B
Founded: 1903 (as the Compression Rheostat Company)
Employees: 21,000
Website: http://www.rockwell.com
Address: (U.S.)
Rockwell Automation, Inc.
1201 South Second Street
Milwaukee, WI 53204
Phone: (414) 382-2000
Investor Relations:
Phone: (414) 382-8410
E-mail: shareownerrelations@ra.rockwell.com
Company Summary: Rockwell Automation, Inc. is a provider of industrial automation, power, control and information solutions.

Revenue (Millions $)

Year	1st Q	2nd Q	3rd Q	4th Q	Year Total
2008:	1,331	1,407	1,475	1,484	5,697
2009:	1,189	1,058	1,011	1,074	4,332
2010:	1,067	1,165	1,268	1,357	4,857
2011:	1,366	1,464	1,516	1,654	6,000
2012:	1,473	—	—	—	—

Dividends (per share-last four)

$	Date Declared	Ex-Dividend Date	Date of Record	Payment Date
.35	04/06/11	05/12/11	05/16/11	06/10/11
.425	06/02/11	08/11/11	08/15/11	09/12/11
.425	11/02/11	11/09/11	11/14/11	12/12/11
.425	02/08/12	02/16/12	02/21/12	03/12/12

SEMPRA ENERGY

Symbol: SRE (NYSE)
Price: $56.90 (as of 01/31/12)
Ratings:
   The Street: BUY
   Standard & Poor's: BUY ★ ★ ★ ★
   Ford Equity Research: BUY
Sector: Utilities
Industry: Gas and Electric Utilities
52-Week Range: $44.78 (08/09/11)-Low
                   $58.42 (01/26/12)-High
Shares Outstanding: 239.91M
Beta: .38
P/E (Trailing 12-Month): $10.25
EPS (Trailing 12-Month): $5.55
Annual Dividend per Share and Yield: $1.92/3.30%
Market Capitalization: $13.63B
Founded: 1998
Employees: 17,483
Website: http://www.sempra.com
Address: (U.S.)
Sempra Energy
101 Ash Street
San Diego, CA 92101
Phone: (619) 696-2000
Investor Relations:
Phone: (877) 736-7727
E-mail: Investor@Sempra.com

Company Summary: Sempra Energy is a natural gas and electric utility holding company. The company divides its interests into two broad categories: Sempra Utilities, including Pacific Enterprises/Southern California Gas Company and San Diego Gas & Electric; and Sempra Global, a holding company for businesses not subject to California utilities regulation.

Revenue (Millions $)

Year	1st Q	2nd Q	3rd Q	4th Q	Year Total
2008:	3,270	2,503	2,692	2,293	10,758
2009:	2,108	1,689	1,853	2,456	8,106
2010:	2,534	2,008	2,116	2,345	9,003
2011:	2,434	2,422	2,576	2,604	10,036

Dividends (per share-last four)

$	Date Declared	Ex-Dividend Date	Date of Record	Payment Date
.48	06/14/11	06/22/11	06/24/11	07/15/11
.48	09/13/11	09/27/11	09/29/11	10/15/11
.48	12/06/11	12/20/12	12/22/11	01/15/12
.60	02/24/12	03/22/12	03/26/12	04/15/12

SIGMA-ALDRICH CORP.

Symbol: SIAL (NASDAQ)
Price: $68.04 (as of 01/31/12)
Ratings:
   The Street: BUY
   Standard & Poor's: BUY ★ ★ ★ ★
   Ford Equity Research: HOLD
Sector: Materials
Industry: Specialty Chemicals
52-Week Range: $56.18 (08/08/11)-Low
                   $76.16 (07/07/11)-High
Shares Outstanding: 120.73M
Beta: 1.00
P/E (Trailing 12-Month): $18.90
EPS (Trailing 12-Month): $3.60
Annual Dividend per Share and Yield: $.72/1.10%
Market Capitalization: $8.19B
Founded: 1934 (as Midwest Consultants – parent company of Sigma Chemical Company)
Employees: 8,300
Website: http://www.sigma-aldrich.com
Address: (U.S.)
Sigma-Aldrich Corp.
3050 Spruce Street
St. Louis, MO 63103
Phone: 314-771-5765
Investor Relations:
Phone: (314) 286-8004
E-mail: investorrelations@sial.com
Company Summary: Sigma-Aldrich Corp. is a life science and chemical technology company and engages in development of biochemicals, organic chemicals and chromatography products.

Revenue (Millions $)

Year	1st Q	2nd Q	3rd Q	4th Q	Year Total
2008:	569.6	580.7	540.6	509.8	2,201
2009:	519.3	522.0	533.8	572.0	2,147
2010:	572.0	554.0	563.0	582.0	2,271
2011:	632.0	637.0	626.0	610.0	2,505

Dividends (per share-last four)

$	Date Declared	Ex-Dividend Date	Date of Record	Payment Date
.18	05/03/11	05/27/11	06/01/11	06/15/11
.18	08/10/11	08/30/11	09/01/11	09/15/11
.18	11/08/11	11/29/11	12/01/11	12/15/11
.20	02/14/12	02/28/12	03/01/12	03/15/12

SIMON PROPERTY GROUP, INC.

Symbol: SPG (NYSE)
Price: $135.86 (as of 01/31/12)
Ratings:
    The Street: BUY
    Standard & Poor's: BUY ★ ★ ★ ★
    Ford Equity Research: BUY
Sector: Financials
Industry: Retail REITS
52-Week Range: $99.60 (08/08/11)-Low
                   $137.29 (01/26/12)-High
Shares Outstanding: 297.75M
Beta: 1.51
P/E (Trailing 12-Month): $45.48
EPS (Trailing 12-Month): $2.99
Annual Dividend per Share and Yield: $3.60/2.60%
Market Capitalization: $39.91B
Founded: 1993
Employees: 3,300
Website: http://www.simon.com/
Address: (U.S.)
Simon Property Group, Inc.
225 West Washington Street
Indianapolis, IN 46204
Phone: (317) 636-1600
Investor Relations:
E-mail: IRContact@simon.com
Company Summary: Simon Property Group, Inc. is a commercial real estate company, ranked number one in the United States as the largest real estate investment trust. The company owns or has an interest in 393 properties comprising 264,000,000 square feet leasable area in North America, Europe and Asia.

Revenue (Millions $)

Year	1st Q	2nd Q	3rd Q	4th Q	Year Total
2008:	895.3	922.9	935.6	1,029	3,783
2009:	918.5	903.6	924.9	1,028	3,775
2010:	925.1	933.6	979.3	1,119	3,957
2011:	1,020	1,041	1,074	1,171	4,306

Dividends (per share-last four)

$	Date Declared	Ex-Dividend Date	Date of Record	Payment Date
.80	07/26/11	08/15/11	08/17/11	08/31/11
.90	10/25/11	11/14/11	11/16/11	11/30/11
.20	10/25/11	12/14/11	12/16/11	12/30/11
.95	02/03/12	02/13/12	02/15/12	02/29/12

J. M. SMUCKER CO.

Symbol: SJM (NYSE)
Price: $78.78 (as of 01/31/12)
Ratings:
    The Street: BUY
    Standard & Poor's: BUY ★ ★ ★ ★
    Ford Equity Research: HOLD
Sector: Consumer Goods
Industry: Processed and Packaged Foods
52-Week Range: $66.43 (08/26/11)-Low
                   $81.40 (01/25/12)-High
Shares Outstanding: 112.02M
Beta: .54
P/E (Trailing 12-Month): $19.55
EPS (Trailing 12-Month): $4.03
Annual Dividend per Share and Yield: $1.92/2.40%
Market Capitalization: $8.93B
Founded: 1897
Employees: 4,500
Website: http://www.smucker.com
Address: (U.S.)
The J. M. Smucker Co.
One Strawberry Lane
Orrville, OH 44667-0280
Phone: (330) 682-3000
Investor Relations:
Phone: (330) 684-3838
Company Summary: The J. M. Smucker Co. is a manufacturer of fruit spreads, ice cream toppings, beverages, shortening and oils, and health and natural foods.

J. M. Smucker Co. (SJM)

Revenue (Millions $)

Year	1st Q	2nd Q	3rd Q	4th Q	Year Total
2008:	561.5	707.9	665.4	590.0	2,525
2009:	663.7	843.1	1,182	1,068	3,757
2010:	1,051	1,279	1,206	1,069	4,605
2011:	1,047	1,279	1,312	1,187	4,825
2012:	1,189	1,514	1,467	—	—

Dividends (per share-last four)

$	Date Declared	Ex-Dividend Date	Date of Record	Payment Date
.44	04/21/11	05/11/11	05/13/11	06/01/11
.48	07/22/11	08/10/11	08/12/11	09/01/11
.48	10/25/11	11/08/11	11/11/11	12/01/11
.48	01/26/12	02/08/12	02/10/12	03/01/12

SOUTHWEST AIRLINES CO.

Symbol: LUV (NYSE)
Price: $9.58 (as of 01/31/12)
Ratings:
  The Street: BUY
  Standard & Poor's: BUY ★ ★ ★ ★
  Ford Equity Research: BUY
Sector: Industrials
Industry: Regional Airlines
52-Week Range: $7.15 (10/04/11)-Low
            $12.87 (04/01/11)-High
Shares Outstanding: 772.91M
Beta: 1.33
P/E (Trailing 12-Month): $41.65
EPS (Trailing 12-Month): $.23
Annual Dividend per Share and Yield: $.02/.20%
Market Capitalization: $7.44B
Founded: 1967
Employees: 45,392
Website: http://www.southwest.com
Address: (U.S.)
Southwest Airlines Co.
2702 Love Field Drive
P O Box 36611
Dallas, TX 75235-1611
Phone: (214) 792-4000
Investor Relations:
Phone: (214) 792-4415
Company Summary: Southwest Airlines Co. is a low-cost airline and engages primarily in short-haul flights.

Revenue (Millions $)

Year	1st Q	2nd Q	3rd Q	4th Q	Year Total
2008:	2,530	2,869	2,890	2,734	11,023
2009:	2,357	2,615	2,666	2,712	10,350
2010:	2,630	3,168	3,192	3,114	12,104
2011:	3,103	4,136	4,311	4,108	15,658

Dividends (per share-last four)

$	Date Declared	Ex-Dividend Date	Date of Record	Payment Date
.0045	05/18/11	06/06/11	06/08/11	06/22/11
.0045	07/28/11	08/23/11	08/25/11	09/15/11
.0045	11/17/11	12/06/11	12/08/11	01/05/12
.0045	01/26/12	02/28/12	03/01/12	03/22/12

STANLEY BLACK & DECKER, INC.

Symbol: SWK (NYSE)
Price: $70.18 (as of 01/31/12)
Ratings:
    The Street: BUY
    Standard & Poor's: BUY ★ ★ ★ ★
    Ford Equity Research: HOLD
Sector: Industrials
Industry: Machine Tools and Accessories
52-Week Range: $47.07 (10/04/11)-Low
                  $78.19 (04/26/11)-High
Shares Outstanding: 169.55M
Beta: 1.66
P/E (Trailing 12-Month): $18.46
EPS (Trailing 12-Month): $3.80
Annual Dividend per Share and Yield: $1.64/2.30%
Market Capitalization: $11.85B
Founded: 1843 (as Stanley's Bolt Manufactory)
Employees: 44,700
Website: http://www.stanleyblackanddecker.com/
Address: (U.S.)
Stanley Black & Decker, Inc.
1000 Stanley Drive
New Britain, CT 06053
Phone: (860) 225-5111
Investor Relations:
E-mail: investorrelations@swkbdk.com
Company Summary: Stanley Black & Decker, Inc. is a manufacturer of tools and hardware and provider of security products and locks. Stanley Black & Decker, Inc. is the result of the merger of Stanley Works and Black & Decker on March 12, 2010.

Revenue (Millions $)

Year	1st Q	2nd Q	3rd Q	4th Q	Year Total
2008:	1,096	1,131	1,119	1,078	4,426
2009:	913.0	919.2	935.5	914.9	3,683
2010:	1,262	2,365	2,369	2,347	8,343
2011:	2,380	2,623	2,636	2,736	10,376

Dividends (per share-last four)

$	Date Declared	Ex-Dividend Date	Date of Record	Payment Date
.41	04/19/11	05/27/11	06/01/11	06/21/11
.41	07/15/11	08/31/11	09/02/11	09/20/11
.41	10/13/11	11/30/11	12/02/11	12/13/11
.41	02/14/12	03/05/12	03/07/12	03/20/12

THERMO FISHER SCIENTIFIC, INC.

Symbol: TMO (NYSE)
Price: $52.90 (as of 01/31/12)
Ratings:
    The Street: BUY
    Standard & Poor's: BUY ★ ★ ★ ★
    Ford Equity Research: BUY
Sector: Health Care
Industry: Medical Instruments, Supplies and Services
52-Week Range: $43.06 (12/15/11)-Low
                $65.86 (05/31/11)-High
Shares Outstanding: 365.85M
Beta: .45
P/E (Trailing 12-Month): $15.44
EPS (Trailing 12-Month): $3.43
Annual Dividend per Share and Yield: N/A
Market Capitalization: $20.01B
Founded: 2006 (by Merger of Thermo Electron and Fisher Scientific)
Employees: 39,300
Website: http://www.thermofisher.com
Address: (U.S.)
Thermo Fisher Scientific, Inc.
81 Wyman Street
Waltham, MA 02454
Phone: (781) 622-1000
Investor Relations:
Phone: (781) 622-1111
E-mail: investorrelations@thermofisher.com
Company Summary: Thermo Fisher Scientific, Inc. is a health care equipment company that develops and manufactures analytical and laboratory products and services used in health care, scientific research, safety, and education.

Revenue (Millions $)

Year	1st Q	2nd Q	3rd Q	4th Q	Year Total
2008:	2,554	2,710	2,588	2,646	10,498
2009:	2,255	2,484	2,531	2,641	9,911
2010:	2,627	2,596	2,629	2,718	10,570
2011:	2,721	2,897	2,974	3,133	11,725

Dividends (last)

$	Date Declared	Ex-Dividend Date	Date of Record	Payment Date
.13	02/29/12	03/13/12	03/15/12	04/16/12

TIME WARNER, INC.

Symbol: TWX (NYSE)
Price: $37.06 (as of 01/31/12)
Ratings:
    The Street: BUY
    Standard & Poor's: BUY ★ ★ ★ ★
    Ford Equity Research: STRONG BUY
Sector: Consumer Services
Industry: Entertainment
52-Week Range: $27.62 (08/22/11)-Low
                     $38.62 (05/02/11)-High
Shares Outstanding: 969.64M
Beta: 1.22
P/E (Trailing 12-Month): $14.07
EPS (Trailing 12-Month): $2.63
Annual Dividend per Share and Yield: $.94/2.50%
Market Capitalization: $37.09B
Founded: 1990
Employees: 34,000
Website: http://www.timewarner.com
Address: (U.S.)
Time Warner, Inc.
One Time Warner Center
New York, NY 10019-8016
Phone: (212) 484-8000
Investor Relations:
Phone: (866) 463-6899
E-mail: ir@timewarner.com
Company Summary: Time Warner, Inc. is a media company with major operations in film, television and publishing.

Revenue (Millions $)

Year	1st Q	2nd Q	3rd Q	4th Q	Year Total
2008:	11,417	11,555	11,706	12,306	46,984
2009:	5,996	5,920	6,262	7,210	25,388
2010:	6,322	6,377	6,377	7,812	26,888
2011:	6,683	7,030	7,068	8,193	28,974

Dividends (per share-last four)

$	Date Declared	Ex-Dividend Date	Date of Record	Payment Date
.235	04/29/11	05/26/11	05/31/11	06/15/11
.235	07/28/11	08/29/11	08/31/11	09/15/11
.235	10/27/11	11/28/11	11/30/11	12/15/11
.26	02/08/12	02/27/12	02/29/12	03/15/12

TITANIUM METALS CORP.

Symbol: TIE (NYSE)
Price: $15.38 (as of 01/31/12)
Ratings:
> **The Street:** HOLD
> **Standard & Poor's:** BUY ★ ★ ★ ★
> **Ford Equity Research:** HOLD

Sector: Materials
Industry: Industrial Metals
52-Week Range: $13.28 (08/18/11)-Low
$20.39 (05/03/11)-High
Shares Outstanding: 175.18M
Beta: 1.47
P/E (Trailing 12-Month): $25.21
EPS (Trailing 12-Month): $.61
Annual Dividend per Share and Yield: $.30/1.90%
Market Capitalization: $2.69B
Founded: 1950
Employees: 2,750
Website: http://www.timet.com
Address: (U.S.)
Titanium Metals Corp.
5430 Lyndon B. Johnson Freeway
Suite 1700
Dallas, TX 75240
Phone: (972) 233-1700
Investor Relations:
E-mail: investor.relations@timet.com
Company Summary: Titanium Metals Corp. is a manufacturer of titanium-based metal products.

Titanium Metals Corp. (TIE)

Revenue (Millions $)

Year	1st Q	2nd Q	3rd Q	4th Q	Year Total
2008:	293.1	297.3	295.4	265.2	1,151
2009:	203.4	205.7	181.4	183.5	774
2010:	217.5	212.0	210.3	217.3	857
2011:	252.0	272.0	262.5	258.6	1,045

Dividends (per share-last four)

$	Date Declared	Ex-Dividend Date	Date of Record	Payment Date
.075	05/17/11	06/08/11	06/10/11	06/21/11
.075	08/01/11	09/07/11	09/09/11	09/20/11
.075	10/27/11	12/07/11	12/09/11	12/20/11
.075	02/16/12	03/07/12	03/09/12	03/21/12

UNITED PARCEL SERVICE, INC.

Symbol: UPS (NYSE)
Price: $75.65 (as of 01/31/12)
Ratings:
   The Street: BUY
   Standard & Poor's: BUY ★ ★ ★ ★
   Ford Equity Research: BUY
Sector: Industrials
Industry: Air Freight and Logistics
52-Week Range: $60.74 (08/09/11)-Low
$77.00 (02/18/11)-High
Shares Outstanding: 958.72M
Beta: 1.05
P/E (Trailing 12-Month): $18.36
EPS (Trailing 12-Month): $4.12
Annual Dividend per Share and Yield: $2.08/2.70%
Market Capitalization: $73.00B
Founded: 1907
Employees: 222,020 (full-time)
Website: http://www.ups.com
Address: (U.S.)
United Parcel Service, Inc.
55 Glenlake Parkway NE
Atlanta, GA 30328
Phone: (404) 828-6000
Investor Relations:
Phone: (404) 828-6000
Company Summary: United Parcel Service, Inc. is a package delivery company that on average delivers more than 15 million packages a day in more than 220 countries and territories.

Revenue (Millions $)

Year	1st Q	2nd Q	3rd Q	4th Q	Year Total
2008:	12,675	13,001	13,113	12,697	51,486
2009:	10,938	10,829	11,153	12,377	45,297
2010:	11,728	12,204	12,192	13,421	49,545
2011:	12,582	13,191	13,166	14,166	53,105

Dividends (per share-last four)

$	Date Declared	Ex-Dividend Date	Date of Record	Payment Date
.52	05/05/11	05/12/11	05/16/11	06/01/11
.52	08/11/11	08/18/11	08/22/11	09/07/11
.52	11/07/11	11/09/11	11/14/11	11/30/11
.57	02/09/12	02/16/12	02/21/12	03/07/12

U.S. BANCORP
Symbol: USB (NYSE)
Price: $28.22 (as of 01/31/12)
Ratings:
   The Street: BUY
   Standard & Poor's: HOLD ★ ★ ★
   Ford Equity Research: BUY
Sector: Financials
Industry: Banking
52-Week Range: $20.10 (08/23/11)-Low
              $29.42 (01/17/12)-High
Shares Outstanding: 1.91B
Beta: 1.23
P/E (Trailing 12-Month): $11.47
EPS (Trailing 12-Month): $2.46
Annual Dividend per Share and Yield: $.50/1.80%
Market Capitalization: $53.90B
Founded: 1929
Employees: 62,529
Website: http://www.usbank.com
Address: (U.S.)
U.S. Bancorp
800 Nicollet Mall
Minneapolis, MN 55402
Phone: (651) 466-3000
Investor Relations:
Phone: (866) 775-9668
E-mail: judith.murphy@usbank.com
Company Summary: U.S. Bancorp is a financial services holding company and is the parent company of U.S. Bank, the fifth largest commercial bank in the United States based on assets of $340 billion.

Revenue (Millions $)

Year	1st Q	2nd Q	3rd Q	4th Q	Year Total
2008:	5,500	4,970	4,880	4,857	20,207
2009:	4,655	4,895	4,950	4,990	19,490
2010:	4,911	5,105	5,187	5,315	20,518
2011:	5,112	5,265	5,371	5,651	21,399

Dividends (per share-last four)

$	Date Declared	Ex-Dividend Date	Date of Record	Payment Date
.125	06/21/11	06/28/11	06/30/11	07/15/11
.125	09/20/11	09/28/11	09/30/11	10/17/11
.125	12/13/11	12/28/11	12/30/11	01/17/12
.195	03/13/12	03/28/12	03/30/12	04/16/12

UNITED TECHNOLOGIES CORP.
Symbol: UTX (NYSE)
Price: $78.35 (as of 01/31/12)
Ratings:
  The Street: BUY
  Standard & Poor's: HOLD ★ ★ ★
  Ford Equity Research: HOLD
Sector: Industrials
Industry: Aerospace and Defense
52-Week Range: $66.87 (10/04/11)-Low
  $91.83 (07/07/11)-High
Shares Outstanding: 908.86M
Beta: 1.15
P/E (Trailing 12-Month): $14.27
EPS (Trailing 12-Month): $5.49
Annual Dividend per Share and Yield: $1.92/2.50%
Market Capitalization: $69.57B
Founded: 1934 (as United Aircraft Corp.)
Employees: 199,900
Website: http://www.utc.com
Address: (U.S.)
United Technologies Corp.
One Financial Plaza
United Technologies Building
Hartford, CT 06101
Phone: (860) 728-7000
Investor Relations:
Phone: (860) 728-7608
E-mail: invrelations@corphq.utc.com
Company Summary: United Technologies Corp. researches, develops, and manufactures high-technology products such as aircraft engines, helicopters, HVAC, fuel cells, elevators and escalators, fire and security building systems, and industrial products.

Revenue (Millions $)

Year	1st Q	2nd Q	3rd Q	4th Q	Year Total
2008:	13,701	15,667	14,814	14,499	58,681
2009:	12,199	13,060	13,187	13,979	52,425
2010:	12,040	13,802	13,620	14,864	54,326
2011:	13,344	15,076	14,804	14,966	58,190

Dividends (per share-last four)

$	Date Declared	Ex-Dividend Date	Date of Record	Payment Date
.48	04/13/11	05/18/11	05/20/11	06/10/11
.48	06/08/11	08/17/11	08/19/11	09/10/11
.48	10/12/11	11/16/11	11/18/11	12/10/11
.48	02/06/12	02/15/12	02/17/12	03/10/12

VERIZON COMMUNICATIONS, INC.

Symbol: VZ (NYSE)
Price: $37.66 (as of 01/31/12)
Ratings:
  The Street: BUY
  Standard & Poor's: HOLD ★ ★ ★ ☆ ☆
  Ford Equity Research: HOLD
Sector: Telecommunication Services
Industry: Telecommunication Services
52-Week Range: $32.28 (08/09/11)-Low
  $40.48 (01/03/12)-High
Shares Outstanding: 2.84B
Beta: .52
P/E (Trailing 12-Month): $44.31
EPS (Trailing 12-Month): $.85
Annual Dividend per Share and Yield: $2.00/5.40%
Market Capitalization: $106.73B
Founded: 1983
Employees: 193,900
Website: http://www.verizon.com
Address: (U.S.)
Verizon Communications, Inc.
140 West Street
New York, NY 10007
Phone: (212) 395-1000
Investor Relations:
E-mail: kevin.r.tarrant@verizon.com
Company Summary: Verizon Communications, Inc. is a broadband and telecommunications company and offers wireline, wireless, internet, digital television and network services.

Revenue (Millions $)

Year	1st Q	2nd Q	3rd Q	4th Q	Year Total
2008:	23,833	24,124	24,752	24,645	97,354
2009:	26,591	26,861	27,265	27,091	107,808
2010:	26,913	26,773	26,484	26,395	106,565
2011:	26,990	27,536	27,913	28,436	110,875

Dividends (per share-last four)

$	Date Declared	Ex-Dividend Date	Date of Record	Payment Date
.4875	06/02/11	07/06/11	07/08/11	08/01/11
.50	09/01/11	10/05/11	10/07/11	11/01/11
.50	12/01/11	01/06/12	01/10/12	02/01/12
.50	03/02/12	04/05/12	04/10/12	05/01/12

V. F. CORP.

Symbol: VFC (NYSE)
Price: $131.49 (as of 01/31/12)
Ratings:

The Street: BUY
Standard & Poor's: BUY ★ ★ ★ ★
Ford Equity Research: HOLD

Sector: Consumer Goods
Industry: Textiles and Accessories
52-Week Range: $91.60 (06/08/11)-Low
$142.50 (10/31/11)-High
Shares Outstanding: 110.60M
Beta: .81
P/E (Trailing 12-Month): $21.23
EPS (Trailing 12-Month): $6.20
Annual Dividend per Share and Yield: $2.88/2.20%
Market Capitalization: $14.51B
Founded: 1899
Employees: 58,000
Website: http://www.vfc.com
Address: (U.S.)
V. F. Corp.
105 Corporate Center Boulevard
Greensboro, NC 27408
Phone: (336) 424-6000
Investor Relations:
E-mail: irrequest@vfc.com
Company Summary: VF Corp. is an apparel company that sells jeanswear, intimate apparel, daypacks, and workwear.

Revenue (Millions $)

Year	1st Q	2nd Q	3rd Q	4th Q	Year Total
2008:	1,846	1,677	2,207	1,912	7,643
2009:	1,725	1,486	2,094	1,915	7,220
2010:	1,750	1,594	2,232	2,126	7,703
2011:	1,959	1,840	2,750	2,910	9,459

Dividends (per share-last four)

$	Date Declared	Ex-Dividend Date	Date of Record	Payment Date
.63	04/29/11	06/08/11	06/10/11	06/20/11
.63	07/21/11	09/07/11	09/09/11	09/19/11
.72	10/24/11	12/07/11	12/09/11	12/19/11
.72	02/16/12	03/07/12	03/09/12	03/19/12

WALGREEN CO.

Symbol: WAG (NYSE)
Price: $33.36 (as of 01/31/12)
Ratings:
   The Street: BUY
   Standard & Poor's: BUY ★ ★ ★ ★
   Ford Equity Research: HOLD
Sector: Consumer Goods
Industry: Drug Retail
52-Week Range: $30.34 (11/23/11)-Low
                  $45.34 (06/20/11)-High
Shares Outstanding: 869.30M
Beta: 1.04
P/E (Trailing 12-Month): $11.29
EPS (Trailing 12-Month): $2.96
Annual Dividend per Share and Yield: $.90/2.60%
Market Capitalization: $29.14B
Founded: 1901
Employees: 176,000
Website: http://www.walgreens.com
Address: (U.S.)
Walgreen Co.
108 Wilmot Road
Deerfield, IL 60015
Phone: (847) 315-2500
Investor Relations:
Phone: (847) 315-2361
E-mail: investor.relations@walgreens.com
Company Summary: Walgreen Co. is the largest drug retail chain based on revenues. The company operates 8,270 locations across all 50 states, the District of Columbia and Puerto Rico.

Revenue (Millions $)

Year	1st Q	2nd Q	3rd Q	4th Q	Year Total
2008:	14,027	15,394	15,016	14,597	59,034
2009:	14,947	16,475	16,210	15,703	63,335
2010:	16,364	16,987	17,199	16,870	67,420
2011:	17,344	18,502	18,371	17,967	72,184
2012:	18,157	18,651	—	—	—

Dividends (per share-last four)

$	Date Declared	Ex-Dividend Date	Date of Record	Payment Date
.175	04/11/11	05/18/11	05/20/11	06/11/11
.225	07/13/11	08/17/11	08/19/11	09/12/11
.225	10/12/11	11/09/11	11/14/11	12/12/11
.225	01/12/12	02/15/12	02/17/12	03/12/12

WAL-MART STORES, INC.

Symbol: WMT (NYSE)
Price: $61.36 (as of 01/31/12)
Ratings:

The Street: BUY
Standard & Poor's: BUY ★ ★ ★ ★
Ford Equity Research: HOLD

Sector: Consumer Goods
Industry: Discount Stores
52-Week Range: $48.31 (08/10/11)-Low
$62.00 (01/24/12)-High
Shares Outstanding: 3.40B
Beta: .46
P/E (Trailing 12-Month): $12.99
EPS (Trailing 12-Month): $4.72
Annual Dividend per Share and Yield: $1.46/2.40%
Market Capitalization: $210.14B
Founded: 1962
Employees: 2,200,000
Website: http://www.walmartstores.com
Address: (U.S.)
Wal-Mart Stores, Inc.
702 SW 8th Street
Bentonville, AR 72716
Phone: (479) 273-4000
Investor Relations:
Phone: (479) 273-6463
Company Summary: Wal-Mart Stores, Inc. is a retail company that operates a chain of large discount department and warehouse stores. The company is the largest private employer in the world with over 2 million employees, and is the largest retailer in North America.

Revenue (Millions $)

Year	1st Q	2nd Q	3rd Q	4th Q	Year Total
2008:	86,410	93,012	91,949	107,428	378,799
2009:	95,303	102,658	98,530	107,763	404,254
2010:	94,242	100,848	99,373	113,622	408,085
2011:	99,811	103,726	101,952	116,360	421,849
2012:	104,189	109,366	110,226	123,169	446,950

Dividends (per share-last four)

$	Date Declared	Ex-Dividend Date	Date of Record	Payment Date
.365	03/03/11	05/11/11	05/13/11	06/06/11
.365	03/03/11	08/10/11	08/12/11	09/06/11
.365	03/03/11	12/07/11	12/09/11	01/03/12
.3975	03/01/12	03/08/12	03/12/12	04/04/12

WASTE MANAGEMENT, INC.
Symbol: WM (NYSE)
Price: $34.76 (as of 01/31/12)
Ratings:
   The Street: BUY
   Standard & Poor's: HOLD ★ ★ ★
   Ford Equity Research: HOLD
Sector: Industrials
Industry: Environmental Services
52-Week Range: $27.75 (08/09/11)-Low
               $39.69 (05/02/11)-High
Shares Outstanding: 461.37M
Beta: .63
P/E (Trailing 12-Month): $16.94
EPS (Trailing 12-Month): $2.05
Annual Dividend per Share and Yield: $1.36/3.90%
Market Capitalization: $16.00B
Founded: 1894
Employees: 42,800
Website: http://www.wm.com
Address: (U.S.)
Waste Management, Inc.
1001 Fannin Street
Suite 4000
Houston, TX 77002
Phone: (713) 512-6200
Investor Relations:
Phone: (713) 265-1656
E-mail: eegl@wm.com
Company Summary: Waste Management, Inc. is a waste management and environmental services company.

Revenue (Millions $)

Year	1st Q	2nd Q	3rd Q	4th Q	Year Total
2008:	3,266	3,489	3,525	3,108	13,388
2009:	2,810	2,952	3,023	3,006	11,791
2010:	2,935	3,158	3,235	3,187	12,515
2011:	3,103	3,347	3,522	3,406	13,378

Dividends (per share-last four)

$	Date Declared	Ex-Dividend Date	Date of Record	Payment Date
.34	05/13/11	05/31/11	06/02/11	06/17/11
.34	08/23/11	09/01/11	09/06/11	09/23/11
.34	11/08/11	11/28/11	11/30/11	12/16/11
.355	02/28/12	03/07/12	03/09/12	03/23/12

WATERS CORP.

Symbol: WAT (NYSE)
Price: $86.57 (as of 01/31/12)
Ratings:
> **The Street:** BUY
> **Standard & Poor's:** BUY ★ ★ ★ ★
> **Ford Equity Research:** HOLD

Sector: Health Care
Industry: Life Sciences and Medical Equipment
52-Week Range: $70.88 (12/16/11)-Low
> $100.00 (04/26/11)-High

Shares Outstanding: 89.06M
Beta: .79
P/E (Trailing 12-Month): $18.46
EPS (Trailing 12-Month): $4.69
Annual Dividend per Share and Yield: N/A
Market Capitalization: $7.73B
Founded: 1958 (as Waters Associates)
Employees: 5,672
Website: http://www.waters.com
Address: (U.S.)
Waters Corp.
34 Maple Street
Milford, MA 01757
Phone: (508) 478-2000
Investor Relations:
Phone: (508) 482-2349
E-mail: Gene_Cassis@waters.com
Company Summary: Waters Corp. is an analytical instrument and software company that develops and distributes liquid chromatography, thermal analysis and mass spectrometry products.

Revenue (Millions $)

Year	1st Q	2nd Q	3rd Q	4th Q	Year Total
2008:	371.7	398.8	386.3	418.3	1,575
2009:	333.1	362.8	374.0	428.9	1,499
2010:	367.7	391.1	401.0	483.6	1,643
2011:	427.6	447.6	454.5	521.4	1,851

Dividends (none)

WATSON PHARMACEUTICALS, INC.

Symbol: WPI (NYSE)
Price: $58.63 (as of 01/31/12)
Ratings:
   The Street: BUY
   Standard & Poor's: BUY ★ ★ ★ ★
   Ford Equity Research: BUY
Sector: Health Care
Industry: Pharmaceuticals
52-Week Range: $55.00 (01/24/12)-Low
                 $73.35 (09/20/11)-High
Shares Outstanding: 127.16M
Beta: .13
P/E (Trailing 12-Month): $40.32
EPS (Trailing 12-Month): $1.45
Annual Dividend per Share and Yield: N/A
Market Capitalization: $7.46B
Founded: 1984
Employees: 6,686
Website: http://www.watson.com
Address: (U.S.)
Watson Pharmaceuticals, Inc.
Morris Corporate Center III
400 Interpace Parkway
Parsippany, NJ 07054
Phone: (862) 261-7000
Investor Relations:
Phone: (862) 261-7488
E-mail: investor.relations@watson.com
Company Summary: Watson Pharmaceuticals, Inc. is a pharmaceutical company that produces generic and brand-name drugs.

Revenue (Millions $)

Year	1st Q	2nd Q	3rd Q	4th Q	Year Total
2008:	627.0	622.6	640.7	645.2	2,536
2009:	667.4	677.8	662.1	785.7	2,793
2010:	856.5	875.3	882.4	952.7	3,567
2011:	876.5	1,082	1,082	1,544	4,585

Dividends (none)

WELLS FARGO & CO.

Symbol: WFC (NYSE)
Price: $29.21 (as of 01/31/12)
Ratings:
    The Street: BUY
    Standard & Poor's: BUY ★ ★ ★ ★
    Ford Equity Research: HOLD
Sector: Financials
Industry: Banking
52-Week Range: $22.58 (08/10/11)-Low
                  $34.25 (02/08/11)-High
Shares Outstanding: 5.27B
Beta: 2.00
P/E (Trailing 12-Month)**:** $10.36
EPS (Trailing 12-Month)**:** $2.82
Annual Dividend per Share and Yield: $.48/1.60%
Market Capitalization: $153.72B
Founded: 1852 (as Wells, Fargo & Company)
Employees: 264,200
Website: http://www.wellsfargo.com
Address: (U.S.)
Wells Fargo & Co.
420 Montgomery Street
San Francisco, CA 94104
Phone: (866) 878-5865
Investor Relations:
Phone: (415) 371-2921
Email: investorrelations@wellsfargo.com
Company Summary: Wells Fargo & Co. is a financial services company that engages in banking, insurance, investment, mortgage and consumer finance services.

Wells Fargo & Co. (WFC)

Revenue (Millions $)

Year	1ˢᵗ Q	2ⁿᵈ Q	3ʳᵈ Q	4ᵗʰ Q	Year Total
2008:	13,652	13,728	12,920	12,089	52,389
2009:	23,954	25,044	24,750	24,888	98,636
2010:	23,526	23,417	22,906	23,400	93,249
2011:	22,150	22,092	21,264	22,091	87,597

Dividends (per share-last four)

$	Date Declared	Ex-Dividend Date	Date of Record	Payment Date
.12	07/26/11	08/03/11	08/05/11	09/01/11
.12	10/25/11	11/02/11	11/04/11	12/01/11
.12	01/24/12	02/01/12	02/03/12	03/01/12
.10	03/13/12	03/22/12	03/26/12	03/30/12

WINDSTREAM CORP.

Symbol: WIN (NASDAQ)
Price: $12.06 (as of 01/31/12)
Ratings:
> **The Street:** BUY
> **Standard & Poor's:** STRONG BUY ★ ★ ★ ★
> **Ford Equity Research:** HOLD

Sector: Telecommunication Services
Industry: Telecommunication Services
52-Week Range: $10.76 (08/08/11)-Low
$13.57 (05/20/11)-High
Shares Outstanding: 586.47M
Beta: .71
P/E (Trailing 12-Month): $23.47
EPS (Trailing 12-Month): $.51
Annual Dividend per Share and Yield: $1.00/8.30%
Market Capitalization: $6.22B
Founded: 2006
Employees: 14,638
Website: http://www.windstream.com
Address: (U.S.)
Windstream Corp.
4001 Rodney Parham Road
Little Rock, AR 72212
Phone: (501) 748-7000
Investor Relations:
Phone: (866) 320-7922
E-mail: genesis.white@windstream.com
Company Summary: Windstream Corp. is a provider of voice and data network communications and managed services to businesses in the United States.

Revenue (Millions $)

Year	1st Q	2nd Q	3rd Q	4th Q	Year Total
2008:	811.7	788.2	794.1	777.5	3,172
2009:	755.0	752.9	734.3	754.4	2,997
2010:	847.9	917.3	965.8	979.7	3,711
2011:	1,023	1,030	1,023	1,208	4,285

Dividends (per share-last four)

$	Date Declared	Ex-Dividend Date	Date of Record	Payment Date
.25	05/04/11	06/28/11	06/30/11	07/15/11
.25	08/03/11	09/28/11	09/30/11	10/17/11
.25	11/02/11	12/28/11	12/30/11	01/17/12
.25	02/08/12	03/28/12	03/30/12	04/16/12

WYNN RESORTS LTD.

Symbol: WYNN (NASDAQ)
Price: $115.23 (as of 01/31/12)
Ratings:
    The Street: BUY
    Standard & Poor's: BUY ★ ★ ★ ★
    Ford Equity Research: HOLD
Sector: Consumer Services
Industry: Casinos and Resorts
52-Week Range: $101.02 (12/15/11)-Low
                  $172.58 (07/19/11)-High
Shares Outstanding: 124.29M
Beta: 2.45
P/E (Trailing 12-Month): $26.90
EPS (Trailing 12-Month): $4.28
Annual Dividend per Share and Yield: $2.00/1.70%
Market Capitalization: $14.31B
Founded: 2002
Employees: 16,400
Website: http://www.wynnresorts.com
Address: (U.S.)
Wynn Resorts Ltd.
3131 Las Vegas Boulevard South
Las Vegas, NV 89109
Phone: (702) 770-7555
Investor Relations:
Phone: (702) 770-7555
E-mail: investorrelations@wynnresorts.com
Company Summary: Wynn Resorts Ltd. is a developer and operator of hotels and casinos.

Revenue (Millions $)

Year	1st Q	2nd Q	3rd Q	4th Q	Year Total
2008:	778.7	825.2	769.2	614.3	2,987
2009:	740.0	723.3	773.1	809.3	3,046
2010:	908.9	1,033	1,006	1,237	4,185
2011:	1,260	1,367	1,298	1,343	5,269

Dividends (per share-last four)

$	Date Declared	Ex-Dividend Date	Date of Record	Payment Date
.50	07/14/11	07/26/11	07/28/11	08/11/11
.50	10/19/11	10/31/11	11/02/11	11/16/11
5.00	11/01/11	11/21/11	11/23/11	12/21/11
.50	02/02/12	02/14/12	02/16/12	03/01/12

XEROX CORP.

Symbol: XRX (NYSE)
Price: $7.75 (as of 01/31/12)
Ratings:
    The Street: BUY
    Standard & Poor's: HOLD ★ ★ ★ ☆ ☆
    Ford Equity Research: HOLD
Sector: Consumer Goods
Industry: Office Electronics
52-Week Range: $6.55 (10/04/11)-Low
                    $10.99 (04/11/11)-High
Shares Outstanding: 1.33B
Beta: 1.80
P/E (Trailing 12-Month): $8.63
EPS (Trailing 12-Month): $.90
Annual Dividend per Share and Yield: $.17/2.20%
Market Capitalization: $10.36B
Founded: 1906
Employees: 139,650
Website: http://www.xerox.com
Address: (U.S.)
Xerox Corp.
45 Glover Avenue
PO Box 4505
Norwalk, CT 06856-4505
Phone: (203) 968-3000
Investor Relations:
Phone: (203) 849-2656
E-mail: jennifer.horsley@xerox.com
Company Summary: Xerox Corp. is a document management company that produces and sells color and black-and-white printers, multifunction systems, photo copiers, digital production printing presses, and consulting services and supplies.

Revenue (Millions $)

Year	1st Q	2nd Q	3rd Q	4th Q	Year Total
2008:	4,335	4,533	4,370	4,370	17,608
2009:	3,554	3,731	3,675	4,219	15,179
2010:	4,721	5,508	5,428	5,976	21,633
2011:	5,465	5,614	5,583	5,964	22,626

Dividends (per share-last four)

$	Date Declared	Ex-Dividend Date	Date of Record	Payment Date
.0425	05/26/11	06/28/11	06/30/11	07/29/11
.0425	07/14/11	09/28/11	09/30/11	10/31/11
.0425	10/13/11	12/28/11	12/30/11	01/31/12
.0425	02/22/12	03/28/12	03/30/12	04/30/12

YAHOO! INC.

Symbol: YHOO (NASDAQ)
Price: $15.47 (as of 01/31/12)
Ratings:
>**The Street:** BUY
>**Standard & Poor's:** STRONG BUY ★ ★ ★ ★ ★
>**Ford Equity Research:** HOLD

Sector: Information Technology
Industry: Internet Services
52-Week Range: $11.09 (08/08/11)-Low
$18.84 (05/09/11)-High
Shares Outstanding: 1.21B
Beta: .66
P/E (Trailing 12-Month): $18.87
EPS (Trailing 12-Month): $.82
Annual Dividend per Share and Yield: N/A
Market Capitalization: $19.20B
Founded: 1995
Employees: 14,100
Website: http://www.yahoo.com
Address: (U.S.)
Yahoo! Inc.
701 First Avenue
Sunnyvale, CA 94089
Phone: (408) 349-3300
Investor Relations:
E-mail: investor_relations@yahoo-inc.com
Company Summary: Yahoo! Inc. is an internet company and a major provider of online content and services.

Revenue (Millions $)

Year	1st Q	2nd Q	3rd Q	4th Q	Year Total
2008:	1,818	1,798	1,786	1,806	7,208
2009:	1,580	1,573	1,575	1,732	6,460
2010:	1,597	1,601	1,601	1,525	6,324
2011:	1,214	1,229	1,217	1,324	4,984

Dividends (none)

ZIMMER HOLDINGS, INC.

Symbol: ZMH (NYSE)
Price: $60.75 (as of 01/31/12)
Ratings:
 The Street: BUY
 Standard & Poor's: BUY ★ ★ ★ ★
 Ford Equity Research: BUY
Sector: Health Care
Industry: Health Care Equipment
52-Week Range: $47.00 (12/14/11)-Low
 $69.93 (05/11/11)-High
Shares Outstanding: 178.12M
Beta: .90
P/E (Trailing 12-Month): $18.37
EPS (Trailing 12-Month): $3.31
Annual Dividend per Share and Yield: $.72/1.20%
Market Capitalization: $10.88B
Founded: 1927
Employees: 8,700
Website: http://www.zimmer.com
Address: (U.S.)
Zimmer Holdings, Inc.
345 East Main Street
Warsaw, IN 46580
Phone: (574) 267-6131
Investor Relations:
Phone: (574) 267-6131
Company Summary: Zimmer Holdings, Inc. is a medical device company that designs, develops, manufactures and markets orthopedic reconstructive implants, spinal and trauma devices, dental implants, and other related orthopedic surgical products.

Zimmer Holdings, Inc. (ZMH)

Revenue (Millions $)

Year	1st Q	2nd Q	3rd Q	4th Q	Year Total
2008:	1,059	1,080	952.2	1,030	4,121
2009:	992.6	1,020	975.6	1,107	4,095
2010:	1,062	1,058	965.0	1,135	4,220
2011:	1,115	1,137	1,032	1,167	4,451

Dividends (last declared)

$	Date Declared	Ex-Dividend Date	Date of Record	Payment Date
.18	12/19/11	03/28/12	03/30/12	04/27/12